MW01181262

Dear Carr
you and Br
children..
imagine all your feelings right now.
I know God can do miracle — and
that is exactly what I'm praying for
Brad. I'm also praying that you
feel God's presence like never before.

As soon as she hits the stage, Melody Box—everybody's friend—
begins to capture her audience with her goofy, down-to-earth
humor. The audience erupts with laughter. But this time her
script wasn't so funny; and it wasn't a script. It was cancer.
Melody still holds us spellbound as she shares a treasury of
faith in hard times. In this book we hear God's whisper, we
feel His comfort, we rely on His steadiness, and we collapse
into His love. Through the ups and downs of her journey,
Melody joyfully invites us to come and see *He Can Be Trusted*!

SARAH HORNER

God is good, even in the the
most horrific of times. He can
be trusted. I know that to be
true. My husband and I are
praying for you every day. I hope
some of the words in this book are
a comfort & encouragement to you. Melody

What people are saying about this book

Melody Box walked through the fires of adversity and emerged secure in the faithfulness of God. These pages reveal a compelling story of tragedy and triumph, disappointment and satisfaction, cancer and healing—all wrapped up in the goodness and grace of God. You will be greatly blessed and will gain strength from her journey, and you will find the same peace and comfort she has experienced. She is your fellow traveler on the journey of life!

JIMMY DRAPER
President Emeritus
LifeWay Christian Resources

Every one of us goes through hardship and faces dark moments in life. But not everyone points people to Jesus in the middle of their pain! What a privilege to know Melody Box and to be so personally encouraged by her faith in the midst of cancer. *He Can Be Trusted* is inspiring and life changing to the person with eyes to see and a heart to learn from Melody!

SUSAN THOMAS
Author of *Girlfriend Revolution* and *The Best Life*
www.passionatelife.com

I don't know when something has pleased me more than the opportunity to recommended this book written and lived by my dear friend, Melody Box. I have known Melody for more years than I care to admit. She is one of the funniest and wittiest people on the entire planet. But she is also one of the deepest and wisest people on the planet. In November 2005, Melody was the person whom God sovereignly chose to be with me when I got the news that my precious father, Dr. Adrian Rogers, was going into the hospital, never to leave again. She was the one God chose to hold my hand and give me courage. God selected her for a reason. Melody knew the truths of this book before she ever had to live them herself. Sometimes when we have to live out what we have taught to others, it isn't quite the same. But when Melody was again chosen by God, this time to live out these principles in her own life, she lived them as a champion, as a hero of the faith. This book is gripping. Melody is still one of the funniest people on the planet, but it is not just her humor that makes her great. Your life will be changed by reading her story. I know that mine has been changed by being her friend.

GAYLE ROGERS FOSTER
Diamond Executive Director
Premier Designs Jewelry

Having the honor of being friends with Melody Box and walking alongside her through her cancer journey brings reading *He Can Be Trusted* to another dimension for me. I can confidently say that Melody absolutely nails her attempt at putting her journey into words. She has an amazing gift of sharing spiritual insights and wisdom mixed with a healthy dose of humor. Her conversational writing style really makes it feel like you're sitting down to coffee with a friend. You will laugh, cry, and be inspired by Melody's story. Most importantly, you'll be reminded that He really can be trusted, even in the hardest of circumstances.

MICHELLE WESTFALL
Self-Appointed President
Melody Box Fan Club

Can God be trusted when life delivers us a message or condition we do not want? Melody Box speaks from her experience with cancer and her faith in God to answer this question and to give encouragement for every circumstance. Reading *He Can Be Trusted* will bolster your faith and lift your spirits! You will find it meaningful for personal devotions and inspiration!

CLAUDE THOMAS
President of C3Global
Grapevine, Texas

HE CAN BE
Trusted

Discovering God's Presence in
Your Darkest Moments

MELODY BOX

He Can Be Trusted: Discovering God's Presence in Your Darkest Moments
Copyright © 2017 Melody Box

ISBN: 978-1-64085-046-0 Paperback
ISBN: 978-1-64085-048-4 Hardback

First Edition printed 2017

Author Academy Elite
PO Box 43
Powell, Ohio 43035
www.AuthorAcademyElite.com

Printed in the United States of America

DEDICATION

To my family—

To Paul, for marrying Meredith, for giving me two grandchildren, for believing in me.

To Mary, for marrying Matthew, for being my driver, for believing in me.

To Phillip, for marrying Kathryn, for taking the world's best family selfies, for believing in me.

To Meredith, Matthew, and Kathryn. You get me. And you believe in me.

To Phil, for marrying me, for loving me, for taking care of me, for laying down your life for me, for encouraging me, for never giving up on me, for laughing with me, for praying with me, for believing in me. This book would never have been written without you.

CONTENTS

Section One
God Sees You

Section Two
God Hears You

Section Three
God Cares for You

FOREWORD

Melody Box makes me laugh like no other person I know. She can be telling a joke, performing one of her hilarious characters, or just sharing an experience with me. Whatever the situation, the more she talks and acts out the experience, I feel like I'm right there in the room with her and the "funny" is happening to me! If you have ever had the pleasure to hear her tell one of her stories, you know exactly what I mean.

I've had the opportunity to hear Melody speak to audiences of thousands of people, inspiring them to be the best they can be. While she easily commands the stage, she also speaks in such a comfortable, conversational style that everyone instantly feels like she is their best friend. Melody conveys a vulnerability that says, "I've been there, too." And, of course, she makes you laugh until your sides hurt!

We've known each other for more than 25 years and have stayed close through four moves over four states. Our kids have grown up together, and we've all become one big happy family, celebrating weddings and baby showers together. It was when we were planning her daughter's wedding that the discovery was made.

Right smack-dab in the middle of a life of fun came a diagnosis that would knock anyone off their feet. It was rare. It was debilitating. It was life-changing.

I am thrilled to write the foreword for *He Can Be Trusted*. I have been excited about this book ever since Melody sat in my living room and whispered, "I'm going to write a book." In all the years I've known her, I've seen her in many roles— wife, mother, ministry leader, business entrepreneur, and, of course, dear friend. I've watched her go through fun times, ordinary times, and desperate times. She has survived and thrived during all of these seasons because of her deep love for and devotion to Jesus Christ.

Things that would have destroyed most families fueled Melody to push through with enormous integrity, character, and wit. Her faith has strengthened my faith and encouraged me countless times in our friendship. This book will challenge you, inspire you, bless you, and give you a strong desire to excel in all you do.

Melody has a marvelous gift of painting word pictures inspired by her experiences to give real-life applications to her audience. You will laugh and cry as you read her story, and most of all, you will hear God's voice speak to you no matter where you are in your life today!

Enjoy, laugh, and be blessed by this wonderful book, *He Can Be Trusted*.

Elizabeth Draper
2017

ACKNOWLEDGEMENTS

He Can Be Trusted would never have been *conceived* had it not been for the many people telling me, "You should write a book!" or "I'll be first in line when you write your book!" or "Please tell me you are putting all of this in a book!" Thank you, Facebook friends and Premier Designs family. Thank you for messaging me at just the right moments—the moments when I was unsure if I had anything of value to write. Your encouragement to go for it was invaluable.

He Can Be Trusted would never have been *written* without the constant encouragement of my family. There were nights (many nights) when I cried and asked my husband, Phil, to tell me again why I was trying to write a book. There were even more nights when I couldn't get my thoughts together, and Phil talked me through the rough patches. And then there was the face—the face of pure admiration when he read a chapter. Thank you, Phil, for loving me the way you do, believing in me every step of the way, and gently nudging me toward the finish line.

Thank you, Paul and Meredith, Mary and Matt, and Phillip and Kathryn—our precious kids. Your belief that I could do anything inspired me to make you proud. (The hilarious videos you sent to me will be in my mind forever!) I think of your prayers for me, not just through the writing of this book but also through our cancer journey, and I'm in awe of your passion, commitment, and love for the Lord and for me. You are all unbelievable blessings to me.

Thank you to my grandchildren, Emma Jo and Davis. (I just wanted to mention their names so they wouldn't feel left out when they are old enough to read.)

He Can Be Trusted would never have been *published* without my writing and publishing coach, Kary Oberbrunner. His guidance and availability kept me inspired and gave me the courage to do something that I never dreamed I could. Thank you, Kary, for your generosity of time and energy.

Thank you, Carolyn and Michelle, for proofreading the manuscript. Your edits, suggestions, and attention to detail were invaluable to me. (I really liked it when you pointed out the parts that made you laugh or cry.) Thank you, Jenny Morgan, for your final edit of my book. From the moment you agreed to take on the project, I knew God gave you to me. Your delight in wanting to take this on lifted my spirit, and your editing talents have helped make this the best book possible.

He Can Be Trusted would never have been *in your hands* today without two of my favorite cheerleaders and encouragers, Andy and Sarah Horner. I will never forget the phone call and your squeal of excitement when I told you I was going to write a book. Thank you, Sarah, for your timely emails, telling me that the writing was so much in my voice that you could hear me reading it. Your compliments meant the world to me. I love you both so much, and I'm overwhelmed by your support as I walked through my cancer days and my writing days. You are a blessing to me.

Finally, *He Can Be Trusted* would never be able to *shine a light* into your dark moments without the thoughts given to me by my heavenly Father. First and foremost, thank You, Lord, for healing me and giving me more time on this earth with my family and friends. I will never stop thanking You for that. And secondly, thank You for counting me worthy to go through dark times so that You can teach me the lessons in this book. Finally, thank You for loving me and developing in me the character You desire in my life. I love You. I believe in You. And I know You can be trusted.

READ THIS FIRST

My granddaughter, Emma Jo, has captured my heart! For those of you who have grandchildren, an "I told you so" is not needed for me because I knew I would love her and feel captivated by her from the moment my kids told me they were pregnant. I didn't have to see her or hold her to feel this way. I just did.

I even started buying toys for her before she was born. She wouldn't play with or understand these toys for a couple of years, but I wanted to be prepared!

When Emma Jo was about 2 ½ years old, I moved all her toys into my office and created a playroom (or "payroom," as she calls it). When she first saw it, she ooo'd and ahhh'd perfectly. Success! Emma's eyes got big as she looked all around the room, soaking in everything. Now, this is still my office, with my books and pictures on the bookshelf and my computer on the desk. In the corner of the room, I have a mannequin that I use in my business. The mannequin is wearing a little black dress, a jean vest, and some jewelry, but it is basically a PVC pipe with shoulders, no arms, and no head.

Suddenly, I noticed Emma Jo standing perfectly still in the middle of the room, staring at my mannequin. In a small voice, she asked, "What's that?" I realized just then that the mannequin might not be something a 2 ½-year-old would understand. While my mannequin wears a dress and sort of looks like a person, there is something not quite right about her from the eyes of a child. At that time, Emma Jo was going through a phase of being afraid of things that were unfamiliar to her. If one of us wore a funny hat or put on a crazy wig, she didn't like it and would have *nothing* to do with it.

As I saw her little face trying to figure out my mannequin, I thought, "Oh no! I've just ruined the playroom for her!" I tried to answer her question and mumbled something like, "Well, that's Grandma's mannequin. Her name is Mandy." I kept watching Emma Jo, waiting for her to want to be picked up and taken out of the room, when I heard her say quietly, almost under her breath, "I not scared of her." It wasn't a very confident statement. It was more like, "I'm not going to be afraid of that thing that I don't understand because this is *my* playroom. My Grandma is in my playroom, and I want to play in my playroom." She stood there for a few seconds longer, gathering her courage and looking at Mandy. Then she turned and started playing with the tea set on her table.

Whew! I was so proud of her! And so relieved. We played together in the playroom until it was time for her to go home.

The next time Emma Jo came over, she grabbed my hand and said, "Let's go pay in my payroom!" When we walked in, I showed her some new things I had added for her to play with, and then I turned my office chair around to sit in and watch her play. As I sat down, I noticed her standing in front of Mandy the Mannequin, quietly studying her. Without looking at me, Emma Jo reached out, put her hand on my lap, and said, "That's Grandma's Mandy." Because my granddaughter is brilliant and discerning beyond her years, I'm sure she meant, "I'm still a little afraid, and I don't understand her. But if Grandma is here and is okay with this, then I'm going to be okay, too. I'm not going to let my fear of Mandy stop me from playing in my playroom."

This book was written for those of you who have found yourself in a place you are not okay with, a place you don't understand. It may be a financial crisis that shattered the dreams of your future; the loss of an intimate relationship that sent you into a deep depression; or the shocking revelation of a betrayal that left you feeling dazed and deeply wounded. I get it. Unfortunately, none of us will get through life untouched by dark times. The dark time that prompted this book was my stage 4 cancer diagnosis.

When I told my oncologist the name and subtitle of this book, he immediately asked me, "How *do* you discover God's presence in your dark moments?" That's a question we all have, isn't it? We want to know, "Is God near me?" "Does He see what I'm going through?" "Can He hear me crying, and does He even care?"

And many times, we also ask, "Why am *I* going through this?" or "Why is this happening to *me*?" While the answers to the questions in the previous paragraph are a resounding "Yes! God does see, He does hear, He does care," we may never have the answers to the "Why" questions, at least on this side of eternity.

Let me explain it like this: you and a friend walk into an unfamiliar house at night. Suddenly, all the lights go out, and it is so dark you can't see your hand in front of your face. What would comfort you at that moment? An explanation of why the lights went out? "An electric circuit is an unbroken path along which an electric current exists and/or is able to flow. When connections are made properly, the circuit will 'close,' and current will flow through the circuit, causing a lamp to light. When one of the wires is removed from the power source, the circuit is now 'open,' and the lamp will no longer light." How many of you just skimmed that quote? Hey, I wrote it, and even I skimmed over it when I re-read it! My point is that even if God gave you the answer as to why you are going through your dark moment, I don't think it would give you the comfort you seek.

Instead, I believe we find comfort knowing that *we are not alone in the darkness.* Your Friend is right beside you. Discovering God's presence in the midst of your pain is the message of this book. He can be trusted with all your questions, all your fears, all your frustrations, and yes, even all of your doubts. The promises you read in the Bible are not just for biblical times. God is the same yesterday, today, and forever. He does not and cannot change. His purposes and plans WILL be accomplished. They will never be defeated, overthrown, or undone—no matter how bad the darkness gets.

I've chosen to share some stories and Scriptures in this book that helped me get through a particularly dark time in my life. I pray they encourage and comfort you and help you feel not so alone or desperate. Let me assure you: God is never surprised or caught off guard by difficult circumstances. He can be trusted to keep His promise of unconditional love even on the darkest of days.

If I had only one reason to write this book, it would be to tell you that God loves you. He loves you! Infinitely more than you can even comprehend. You may be religious, or you may have no religion. You may have been in church since childhood, or you may have never stepped through the doors of a church in your entire life. Your background doesn't matter to God. YOU matter to Him.

"I've never quit loving you and never will. Expect love, love, and more love!" (Jeremiah 31:3 MSG).

How precious is your unfailing love, O God! All humanity finds shelter in the shadow of your wings (Psalm 36:7).

And I am convinced that nothing can ever separate us from God's love. Neither death nor life, neither angels nor demons,

neither our fears for today nor our worries abo.
not even the powers of hell can separate us fro.
No power in the sky above or in the earth belu
nothing in all creation will ever be able to separate
love of God that is revealed in Christ Jesus our Lora
8:38–39).

I didn't write this book from a position of triumphantly navigating all the difficulties in my life. I've doubted, been discouraged, been afraid, and felt alone, wondering why God was so silent. I've questioned His decisions and tried to convince Him to work a different way in my life. And through my walk through a cancer diagnosis, I cried many tears on my pillow at night. In each of my dark times, God met me, comforted me, and showed me that He *is* faithful and He can *always* be trusted.

It is my sincere desire that as you turn the pages of this book, you also decide to turn your face toward God. God doesn't want you to stand in the darkness feeling all alone. He created you to have a relationship with Him. I would hate for you to waste your time on earth, never experiencing His friendship and His everlasting love for you, or the wonder of how He can bring good out of bad for those who love Him, or how He is faithful and can be trusted to keep His promises.

God loves you, and trying to understand the depth of His love would be like my 2 ½-year-old granddaughter trying to understand how much I love her. It is an impossible task. Nevertheless, (Yeah, I just said "nevertheless." You can do that when you're a writer.) Nevertheless, the truth is that God loves you whether you believe His love or not. He loves you whether you think you are worthy of His love, whether you are angry with Him because of the darkness you are living in, or whether you even doubt His existence. He loves you and accepts you exactly as you are right now. And there is nothing more I can add to that.

"For even if the mountains walk away and the hills fall to pieces, My love won't walk away from you, my covenant commitment of peace won't fall apart" (Isaiah 54:10 MSG).

And we know that God causes everything to work together for the good of those who love God and are called according to his purpose for them (Romans 8:28).

We must hold on to the hope we have, never hesitating to tell people about it. We can trust God to do what he promised (Hebrews 10:23 ERV).

Section One

GOD
SEES YOU

CHAPTER 1

"You're gonna need a bigger boat."

Jaws

L et the stomach gurgling begin. I was invited to a high tea! At a beautiful hotel in Dallas! It was a birthday party for a dear friend, and while I had been invited before and was excited to attend, I was also a little anxious. First of all, I live in Fort Worth. I know how to get around in Fort Worth. Driving in Dallas is a challenge for me. Secondly, it was a *high tea*! So many questions! First: What to wear? Well, I guess that is the only question.

I was anxious. When I found the hotel, I realized I needed to park in the parking garage. (If you ask me, parking garages are only slightly less complicated than a scene from the movie *Inception*). I found a parking spot and then had to figure out what door to go through. I started walking and saw some escalators. At the time, I was walking with a cane and had a brace on my foot, so I wondered if I could handle the fast-moving stairs. I was a little nervous that I would end up like Buddy in *Elf*, with one leg on the stairs and one leg on the landing! I successfully navigated the escalator, and when I got to the top, I surveyed my surroundings to see which way I should go. Aha! I saw revolving doors straight ahead, with the tea room just on the other side. I was in the right place. All I had to do was walk through the atrium to get there. This atrium was circular with cute little shops on the left and the right. In front of the shops were bistro tables arranged in semicircles, all facing the center. To me, it seemed like a rather large opening to walk through, and I wondered why the tables were arranged to have everyone facing that opening.

For a moment, I felt like everyone was looking at me. I decided to dismiss that silly thought. I told myself, "They are *not* watching you. Yes, you are sporting a cane and two different shoes (one that the brace fits in and one very adorable sandal!), but don't get self-conscious and paranoid that people are staring."

So, with all eyes on me, I pulled myself up by my most confident bootstraps and began striding toward the revolving doors that were just beyond the atrium. When I reached the middle of the atrium, I heard a swishing sound at my feet. I looked down, puzzled. Why was there water all around my left shoe? Wait. Why was there water all around both my feet? Where did this water come from? I noticed some holes in the tile. They were in a symmetrical pattern ... Suddenly, the rush of realization came over me. *I was standing. Right. In the middle. Of a fountain!*

The floor I had been walking on gradually sloped down, creating a modern art fountain. No wonder I felt like all eyes were on me—*because they WERE!* Everyone was thinking, "Is that woman going to walk right into the fountain? Yes, she is!" What could I do? At that moment, I would have given anything to be walking with a friend so we could throw our heads back and laugh at our predicament. But no. I was alone. All I could do was take my cane and the pretty birthday gift I was bringing to the high tea and swish out of the fountain, praying the whole time that it didn't start squirting water up in the air!

As I got to the edge of the fountain, my shoes wet and squishy, I thought of the verse in Isaiah:

"When you walk through deep waters, I will be with you. When you go through rivers of difficulty, you will not drown" *(Isaiah 43:2).*

Not funny then. A little funny now. This Scripture has been a favorite of mine for many years and even more so in the past two years as I walked through the deep waters of a cancer diagnosis.

In 2013, I started noticing weakness in my legs when I stepped up on a curb. It wasn't painful, just weak. I didn't think much about it, but my husband, Phil, insisted that I see a doctor. Because of my previous neck and back problems and the MRI's I had already completed, we knew I didn't have any structural problems—no pinched nerves, no bulging discs. So, we went to my neurologist. He treated the weakness with steroids, which helped a little. In the meantime, Phil pressed me to make an appointment at UT Southwestern Medical Clinic, one of the top hospitals in Texas. It took a few months and one hit-and-miss to get in, but we finally met with a doctor who took my issue seriously and started working to resolve it.

After lots of tests, steroid infusions, and incorrect diagnoses, as well as multiple biopsies on my leg and several stays in the hospital, a picture began to develop. We consulted yet another specialist, and per doctor's orders, I stopped all medications. The pain was even worse now. After another test, a radiologist found a tumor at the base of my spine. The tumor had been there a while, but the steroids kept it small.

Until the steroids stopped working. The tumor was growing fast, and it wrapped all around the nerve bundle at the base of my spine. There was no way to remove it. It was even dangerous to get a biopsy of it. If my surgeon hit or nicked any of those nerves, it could affect anything below my waist. After a four-hour MRI to determine the size of the tumor, a four-hour biopsy was scheduled. Immediately after that surgery, we finally had a confirmed diagnosis: Stage 4 Central Nervous System Lymphoma.

Now I was walking in *deep waters*. I was surrounded by rivers of difficulty. But I also knew that God made a promise in that verse in Isaiah that He would be with me. I would not drown.

"Do not be afraid."

"Don't be afraid" is everywhere in the Bible.

"Don't be afraid, for I am with you."[1]
"Don't be afraid. I am here to help you."[2]
"Don't be afraid, for I will be with you and will protect you."[3]
"Don't be afraid, your request has been heard in heaven."[4]
"Don't be afraid, for you are very precious to God."[5]
"Don't be afraid; you are more valuable to God than a whole flock of sparrows."[6]
"Don't be afraid, I am here!"[7]
"Don't be afraid, for you have found favor with God!"[8]
"Don't be afraid! I am the First and the Last."[9]

And there are so many more! Do you get the picture that God wants us not to be afraid because He is with us and He loves us?

Isaiah 43:1 gives three reasons why we should not be afraid because He is with us and loves us.

"I have ransomed you."

God tells us not to fear because He has ransomed us. In other words, He has rescued you by paying the price demanded. He doesn't say, "I will ransom you when you get your life straightened out." Or "I might ransom you if you prove yourself worthy of My payment." He doesn't even say, "I won't ransom you because I know all the things you've done against Me." Instead, God says *He has already paid the ransom for you!* He has ransomed you knowing all the things you have done and all the things you haven't done. You are free!

So, what is holding you captive? I could have easily believed that I was held captive by my diagnosis. My cancer was so rare that when I asked my oncologist what my prognosis was, he just looked at me, shrugged his shoulders, and said, "We don't know. We've not seen this often enough. Your case is unusual, so we are just going to try the treatment we think might work." While that was frustrating for me to hear because I wanted some certainty about *something*, Phil and my friends reminded me that I didn't have to be afraid because God knew my prognosis.

Maybe you are held captive by a disease or physical limitation. You believe that you are a victim of fate, and now you just have to suck it up and try to get the best you can out of life before time runs out. That's a sad, stifling way to live. God says in Jeremiah 29:11, *"For I know the plans I have for you,"* says the Lord. *"They are plans for good and not for disaster, to give you a future and a hope."*

Psalm 139:16-17 says, *"You saw me before I was born. Every day of my life was recorded in your book. Every moment was laid out before a single day had passed. How precious are your thoughts about me, O God. They cannot be numbered!"*

God knows your days. He knows your path. He knows every moment of your life, and He knew all of this even before you were born! Every moment is precious to Him. What a comfort! This means that I'm not a victim of circumstance, and neither are you. You can trust God. He is the Master Planner of your life.

Maybe you are being held captive by this world's view of success. You are striving for the next promotion, the next award, the next recognition. That is a trap—one that says you are not good enough until you reach whatever it is that is just beyond your grasp. God calls this prideful ambition. The Bible says in Psalm 137:4 (ESV), *"Delight yourself in the Lord, and he will give you the desires of your heart."*

Are you delighting yourself in the things God delights in? Did you know that He does not care one bit about titles or promotions? He cares about *you* and how you will live your life, giving glory to Him in everything. When He is first place in your life, His desires for you become your desires. Then you become a picture to the world that God can be trusted with your dreams and desires, your aspirations and ambitions.

Maybe you have a sin, a habit, or a failure that is holding you back. You think you can never overcome that habit or be forgiven of that failure. 1 John 1:9 promises, *"But if we confess our sins to him, he is faithful and just to forgive us our sins and to cleanse us from all wickedness."*

You can trust Him to forgive. Even if you are not faithful, He *is* faithful.

Are you in bondage to a fear of the future and the "what ifs" of life? Psalm 118:6 says, *"The Lord is for me, so I will have no fear. What can mere people do to me?"* God can be trusted because He is FOR you!

Are you hanging onto a hurt? You've promised yourself that you will *never* be hurt like that again, so you keep your feelings, your love, your affection, and your forgiveness pulled in and protected. No one will ever know the real you, but you convince yourself that's ok. Here is the truth from Matthew 10:39, *"If you cling to your life, you will lose it, but if you give up your life for me, you will find it."*

God says don't be afraid—He has ransomed you! There is nothing so bad, so tragic, so sinful, or so fearful in your life that can keep you from God. The only thing you need to do is accept His payment and release your life completely to Him. When you refuse to give it up to Him and keep holding onto your private sin, your past hurt, and your prideful ambition, you are living in a jail with the doors unlocked and wide-open to freedom. God says you don't have to be afraid—He has delivered you!

And because He knows you, there is nothing hidden from Him. *He knows your special brand of bondage.* We all have something. He ransomed you even while knowing every single thing that you think you have kept hidden from everyone, including Him. This truth is repeated in Romans 5:6-8, *When we were utterly helpless, Christ came at just the right time and died for us sinners. Now, most people would not be willing to die for an upright person, though someone might perhaps be willing to die for a person who is especially good. But God showed his great love for us by sending Christ to die for us while we were still sinners.*

Isn't that amazing?!

Has there ever been a time in your life when you just said, "I give up. I can't do it anymore!"? Maybe you need to give it all to Him right now. Go ahead; put the book aside and pray a prayer like this:

Dear God, I've been fearful and prideful. I've been living like I don't need You to handle my life. I thought I could do it myself. I realize now that I've made a mess of things. I need You. Please forgive me for my pride and distance from You. I accept Your love and forgiveness, and now I give You my life. I want You to be the Lord over everything in my life.

That's it! That's all there is to it. When you ask, He answers. That's one of the things I just love about Him.

9

"I have called you by name."

There is no sweeter sound than your own name. I don't remember how old I was when I realized I didn't know my middle name, but as soon as I could, I asked my mom what it was. She said it was "Jo Ann." I said, "Ugh! I don't like that name!" She laughed and said, "Well, you are named after me." Everyone called my mom "Jo." As soon as I heard that, I said, "Ok, I like it then." And I meant it! Our names are important to us. When someone remembers your name, it's a compliment and makes you feel good.

Other people may forget your children's names, but you will never forget them. (Although you may have to go through the whole roll call to get to the right one. On the first day of school, my nephew told his teacher, "My name is Matthew, but my mom calls me JerMatthew." His brother's name is Jeremy.)

Not only has God ransomed you, but *He knows your name.* Jesus confirms this in John 10:3, in a story about sheep and shepherds, *"The gatekeeper opens the gate for him, and the sheep recognize his voice and come to him. He calls his own sheep by name and leads them out."*

Here, Jesus describes the shared sheep pens of the Middle East. Several townspeople would hire a watchman to guard the pen, and they would bring all their flocks together. When it was time for a shepherd to take his flock out, the gatekeeper would let him in, and the shepherd would call out to the sheep that belonged to him. The sheep would recognize his voice and follow him.

Isn't that fascinating? In that time, it was often the youngest in the family who would be the shepherd of the flock. I can just imagine a ten-year-old boy naming each of the sheep in his flock. He would go to the gate and start calling out, "Blackie! Woolie! Up and at 'em! Batman, Spiderman, Wonder Woman! Come on, let's go. John, Paul, George, Ringo! Get over here. We're leaving!" Or something like that.

The point of Jesus' illustration is that God knows your name. There may be another "Melody Box" in the world, but God has a way of saying my name so that I know He means *me*.

"You are mine."

We all have a need to belong. To belong means we are included, accepted, appreciated, valued, known, and loved. In a perfect world, our first sense of belonging comes from the family into which we were born. However, we don't live in a perfect world. You may be thinking, "You've got that right!" For as long as you can remember, you were told by your mom or dad that you didn't fit in. You were born at the wrong time in their lives. They wanted a girl, but they got a boy. Even though you were part of the family, you knew that you weren't wanted, and you never felt like you belonged.

Maybe you were given up for adoption and spent your early years in foster home after foster home. With each move, you dreamed of belonging to someone. From the dark world of physical and emotional abuse, you have some deep scars of neglect and abandonment. You feel invisible and have a hard time connecting with anyone. I pray that you can cry out to God right now and say, "That wasn't fair! I deserved to be loved and cared for. I deserved to belong. I didn't deserve to be ignored or shamed for existing!"

One of my favorite books in the Bible is the book of Psalms. King David (the David of David and Goliath) wrote many of these songs to God. He doesn't "flower up" his thoughts and make them "presentable" to God. He says it just like it is. David was the youngest boy in a large family, and even though he did some great things—killing a lion and a bear while guarding the sheep; killing a ferocious enemy of Israel; being anointed as the future king—he was mostly disregarded and ignored by his family. And even when David faithfully

11

served King Saul, the king abused and plotted against him. Look at what he writes in Psalm 27:4–10:

The one thing I ask of the Lord—the thing I seek most—is to live in the house of the Lord all the days of my life, delighting in the Lord's perfections and meditating in his Temple. For he will conceal me there when troubles come; he will hide me in his sanctuary. He will place me out of reach on a high rock. Then I will hold my head high above my enemies who surround me. At his sanctuary I will offer sacrifices with shouts of joy, singing and praising the Lord with music. Hear me as I pray, O Lord. Be merciful and answer me! My heart has heard you say, "Come and talk with me." and my heart responds, "Lord, I am coming." Do not turn your back on me. Do not reject your servant in anger. You have always been my helper. **Don't leave me now; don't abandon me. O God of my salvation! Even if my father and mother abandon me, the Lord will hold me close.**

David says his greatest desire is to live in the house of God. He wants to belong. He wants to be accepted. He wants to be known. He loves it when he hears God say, "Come talk with me." (Don't you love it when someone is truly interested in the things you are interested in, and they want to talk with you?) David tells God that his heart is wounded when he says, "Even if my father and mother abandon me." I believe David felt invisible in his large family. But in the same breath, he finds acceptance in God's face as he says, "the Lord will hold me close." *The Message* says it this way, *"My father and mother walked out and left me, but God took me in"* (Psalm 27:10 MSG).

God will take you in, too. He will hold you close. He says, "I have ransomed you. I have called you by name. YOU ARE MINE!"

Every week, this sweet little old lady waited in line at the Post Office to buy two stamps. As she came to the counter one day, the postal worker told her, "You know, you don't have to wait in line to buy stamps. You can get them at the machine over there in books of twenty." The little old lady replied, "Yes, but the machine doesn't ask about my arthritis." You belong to God, and because you are His, He cares about your arthritis.

God Sees Me

Knowing that God knows my name and that I am His, comforts me. I like leaving my life in the hands of the One who created me, who knows me, and who sees me. How do I know He sees me? Because of the next verse: *"When you go through deep waters, I will be with you"* (Isaiah 43:2). You might be tempted to think, "Wait … shouldn't that say, '*Since* I have paid the ransom for you, and *since* I know your name, and *since* you are mine, you will *never* have to go through deep waters or rivers of difficulty'?" Or even, "*If* you ever go through deep waters, I will be with you… and *if* you walk through the fire, I will be with you …" The Bible doesn't say that, though, does it?

In this broken world, I'm not sure how much comfort I would have found in reading, "When the sun is bright, the roses are in bloom, and the grass is green on the path that you walk, and when you're living in your truth, I will be with you." God tells us that our comfort can be found in the knowledge that He sees us. He calls us by name. And that name is near and dear to His heart. He claims us as His own, and when we go through difficult times, He is with us. We will not be overcome by the water or consumed by the fire. Psalm 23:4 says, *Even though I walk through the darkest valley, I will not be afraid, for you are close beside me.*

We live in a messed-up world. As much as we all wish that we didn't have to go through difficulties, pain, heartaches, and trials, they are realities of life. However, *God brings good out of bad.* If you never experience a broken heart or never have to navigate through the pain of sin, betrayal, death, disappointment, or fierce trials, then you'll never experience the real closeness and tenderness of God.

After my surgery, the first thing I remember was Phil holding my hand, leaning very close to my face. I asked him the question I didn't yet know the answer to: "Do I have cancer?" He said a simple, soft "Yes." I started crying a little. I asked him, "Do the kids know?" "Yes," he said. "Do my sisters and brother know?" Another *yes*. "Do our friends know?" Again, *yes*. I remember wanting Phil not to be alone with this knowledge, so I was glad others knew.

After some tears, with Phil holding my hand, I said, "Tell me about God." I remember not knowing how to say, "Tell me that God is aware, that God is here, that God cares." But Phil knew exactly what I was asking. He knew I was scared, and he prayed the most comforting prayer over me in that dark recovery room. At that moment, I felt the presence of God. He was with me. He was and is always with me, but He was especially close in that uncertain moment. As close as Phil's breath on my face.

Are you finding comfort in your dark times knowing that God knows your name, that you are His own possession, and that He is with you and sees you? Or are you gripping so tightly to your life, your worries, and your plans that you can't feel His presence walking beside you? Let go and allow Him to make Himself known to you.

There is no raging flood too deep to separate us from God. There is no consuming flame that can destroy His presence. It reminds me of this beautiful passage in Romans,

And I am convinced that nothing can ever separate us from God's love. Neither death nor life, neither angels nor demons, neither our fears for today nor our worries about tomorrow — not even the powers of hell can separate us from God's love. No power in the sky above or in the earth below — indeed, nothing in all creation will ever be able to separate us from the love of God that is revealed in Christ Jesus our Lord (Romans 8:38).

When I was holding onto the promise that God would be with me as I walked through deep waters and rivers of difficulty and that I would not drown, I didn't interpret the verse to mean that I would not die of cancer. I knew God was telling me *I would not be overcome by the trial.* I also knew that whether He healed me or called me home to Him, I was going to trust Him through it all. To be quite honest, I wasn't about to go to heaven and have God ask me, "Why did you waste this trial worried about yourself? I wanted to use your cancer to put you in front of people you would never have met if not for the cancer!"

No matter what, this journey was not going to be about me. It was going to be about God and His majestic, mind-blowing plan for me—the plan that He had written for me while I was in my mother's womb.

CHAPTER 2

"Ground Control to Major Tom"

David Bowie

The biopsy of the tumor in my back was major surgery. I had to lie very still on my back for what seemed like days. Pillows were stuffed all around me, head to foot, to keep me from moving, and it felt like I was in a cocoon. One night, I woke up and didn't know where I was. The medicine was playing with my mind, and while I knew I was in a hospital, I didn't know why. Several different scenarios flooded into my mind in rapid fire succession:

I'm in the hospital. Why? What's going on? Has the apocalypse happened? Has America been attacked? If I look out the window to my right, will I see small fires burning and bombed-out buildings? Am I in a hospital ward with lots of people in one room? If I look to the left, will I see someone with wounds too scary to look at?

Am I in a space pod? Did I jettison away from the earth before it was completely destroyed?

What's wrong with me? Why can't I move my legs? Do I have legs? Was I in an accident? Where is my family? Were they in an accident with me? Is my family alive?

I desperately tried to shake off the fog. *Why can't I figure this out?*

I prayed for the panic to leave, for clarity to come to my mind, for me to "wake up" and find that I was simply having a very weird dream. Then, suddenly, it came to me.

Oh! I have cancer. (I don't know why I was relieved by that, but I was.)

And at almost the same time, I remembered one of my favorite passages in the Bible. Even though I didn't know where I was, God knew. It may have been dark to me, but it wasn't dark to Him.

"I'm an open book to you; even from a distance, you know what I'm thinking. You know when I leave and when I get back; I'm never out of your sight. You know everything I'm going to say before I start the first sentence. I look behind me and you're there, then I look ahead and you're there, too—your reassuring presence coming and going. This is too much, too wonderful—I can't take it all in! Is there any place I can go to avoid your Spirit? to be out of your sight? If I climb to the sky, you're there! If I go underground, you are there! If I flew on morning's wings to the far western horizon, You'd find me in a minute—you're already there waiting! Then I said to myself, "Oh, he even sees me in the dark! At night I'm immersed in the light." It's a fact: darkness isn't dark to you; night and day, darkness and light, they're all the same to you (Psalm 139:1–12 MSG).

In my dark times, He sees me.

17

While writing this morning, I noticed a Facebook post that shared some startling news. A good friend was in an auto accident last night, and at 10:00 p.m., he was instantly taken from us. When I read this, I started vigorously scrolling through other messages, thinking and praying that this was just a story to get people's attention and maybe it was the beginning of a joke—a cruel joke—because my mind wouldn't accept this as truth.

I felt disoriented. Many of us had just spent time with him at a conference the past weekend. Many of us watched him daily on Facebook as he preached and led us in morning worship. Many of us know his family and had been celebrating with his wife and children as they recently announced a new ministry direction for 2017.

And now he was gone?

I felt the same feeling of confusion and fear that I had in the hospital room when I woke up and didn't know where I was. It's a terrible feeling.

I sent a private message to his wife. I had no clue what to say, so I just said what was in my heart:

Francine. I'm in disbelief. I'm so sorry. I know I should be saying things like, "He is rejoicing in heaven right now," but my emotions are just not there yet. I AM praying for you. I miss Wade so much already. I'll try to write more positive things later, but right now, I'm just so sad. I love you.

I know Francine. And I know her children. She will, somehow, get through these dark, terrible days, and God will receive the glory. I'm praying that she will have many moments of relief because even though it is still the truth (I still had cancer, she still lost her beloved), and these are dark times, they are not dark to God. Even though the world is spinning around her and she has feelings of disorientation, God knows exactly where she is. He sees her.

And He sees you. Are you thinking of the dark time you are in right now? A layoff. A miscarriage. A betrayal. An addiction. An illness. Your dark time may be so deep, so profound, that you can't tell a single soul.

This dark time may have caught you off guard, but I can assure you—it did not surprise God. In Psalm 139, David says that God knows everything about him. God knows when David sits, when he stands, when he's on vacation, when he's traveling for business, and when he rests at home. He knows everything David does and everything he says. God knows when David is in a great mood because everything is good, and He knows when he is in the pit of despair (a dark time). He not only knows it, but David even says that God is with him in that dark time!

> *I could ask the darkness to hide me and the light around me to become night—but even in darkness I cannot hide from you (Psalm 139:11-12).*

God is Present, God is Purposeful, and God is Powerful

Three fears can make a dark moment overwhelming: the fear of being alone, the fear of not finding the reason for the darkness, and the fear of no solution, answer, or relief from the darkness. Thankfully, the Bible addresses each of these fears.

He is Present

I can't help but go back to the prophet Isaiah as he instructed the nation of Israel in their dark times of captivity. Isaiah's encouragement to them is also an encouragement to us that God is present during our dark times.

> *O Jacob, how can you say the Lord does not see your troubles? O Israel, how can you say God ignores your rights? Have*

you never heard? Have you never understood? The Lord is the everlasting God, the Creator of all the earth. He never grows weak or weary. No one can measure the depths of his understanding. He gives power to the weak and strength to the powerless. Even youths will become weak and tired, and young men will fall in exhaustion. But those who trust in the Lord will find new strength. They will soar high on wings like eagles. They will run and not grow weary. They will walk and not faint (Isaiah 40:27–31).

What a beautiful passage of promise. Isaiah reminds us that not only does God see us, but He is powerful enough to save us. He does not become overwhelmed by the darkness as humans do, and He has so much understanding of what we are going through that we can't understand His understanding!

He also promises that those who trust in the Lord will find *strength*; they will *soar* (that sounds a lot like being lifted out of a dark place), and they will not *swoon*! (Thank you, thesaurus, for an "s" word that means "faint" to make my illustration work better.)

In the Old Testament, Leah (of the Jacob, Rachel, and Leah fame), is another beautiful example that God is present in our dark times. Leah was the unloved wife, and for most of her life, she was unnoticed by her husband, Jacob. However, while she was unloved and unnoticed by Jacob, it was just the opposite with God.

*When the Lord **saw** that Leah was not loved … (Genesis 29:31 NIV).*

If your dark time is one of feeling unnoticed or unnecessary, the story of Leah in Genesis 29 has some wonderful news. God sees you and looks deep inside your heart and understands your greatest need. When no one else sees, God sees. When no one else cares, God cares. When no one else is present for you, God is present. Leah's deep need was to have children so that her husband would notice her. Three of her first four children were named giving glory to God that He saw her in her dark time.

Reuben: "Look, a son!"—"The Lord has noticed my misery."[10]
Simeon: "One who hears"—"The Lord heard that I was unloved and has given me another son."[11]
Judah: "Praise"—"Now I will praise the Lord!"[12]

After Judah's birth, I can imagine Leah shouting with joy, *"I will praise the Lord as long as I live. I will sing praises to my God with my dying breath[!]"* (Psalm 146:2).

God was present in her time of distress and anguish. She was not alone.

It may *feel* like you are alone in your darkest moments, but we are told not to trust our feelings.

> *"The human heart is the most deceitful of all things, and desperately wicked. Who really knows how bad it is?"* (Jeremiah 17:9).

Feelings come, and feelings go. That's why the Bible says not to live your life dictated by them. It's not a matter of pretending you don't feel a certain way. It is a matter of learning how to manage those feelings and not letting them manage you.

There have been times when I've been insecure about speaking to a group of people, thinking that what I have to say isn't important or impactful. But then I decided to trust God and have the confidence that He would be with me and help me. When I stepped out to speak, those feelings of insecurity tried to creep back into my mind, but I kept trusting in God's promise of His presence and guidance. Soon, my insecurities went away! We can't trust our feelings. But we can trust His promises. Fear has no power in His presence!

21

He is Purposeful

We not only learn from Scripture that we are never alone because of God's presence, but also, we know that there is a purpose for our dark time. God even knew it was coming! Matthew 26:10 says, *"But Jesus, aware of this, replied ... "* He is always aware. I love that!

> *"I don't think the way you think. The way you work isn't the way I work.... For as the sky soars high above the earth, so the way I work surpasses the way you work, and the way I think is beyond the way you think" (Isaiah 55:8–9 MSG).*

That's pretty clear, don't you think? In many cases, we aren't going to be able to figure out everything God is doing in our lives during a dark time, but we can be sure He has a purpose. And within that purpose, He will bring glory to Himself. Whether we understand it or not, we can find comfort knowing that God is in control. No difficulty, tragedy, depression, illness, or dark time can thwart His purpose.

> *"And we know that God causes everything to work together for the good of those who love God and are called according to his purpose for them." (Romans 8:28).*

God works every detail of our lives into something good. He has a bird's-eye view, from beginning to end. When we look at our lives from God's perspective, and when we believe that God is good, then we can see the threads of His goodness, grace, and mercy woven in and around all our dark times. We can see good come out of bad. Anyone can bring good out of good, but only God can bring good out of bad.

He is Powerful

How many of you remember calling out for your mom or your dad in the middle of the night after a bad dream when you were a child? I would call out "Daddy?" softly at first and then louder and louder until he came rushing into my room. I needed to know I wasn't alone. I needed to feel safe knowing he could chase away the fear by telling me, "It was just a bad dream." My dad made me feel *safe*.

One of the great truths of Scripture is that God is powerful. In Genesis 18:10–14, God tells Abraham that he will be a father at the age of 100. His 90-year-old wife, Sarah, laughs, and God asks her a rhetorical question: "*Is anything too difficult for God?*" **Our God is God of the difficult things.**

In Jeremiah 32:27, God speaks to the prophet and says, "*I am the Lord, the God of all the peoples of the world. Is anything too hard for me?*" **Our God is God of the hard places**.

In the oldest book of the Bible, Job answers God with the declaration: "*I'm convinced: You can do anything and everything. Nothing and no one can upset your plans*" (Job 42:2 MSG). **Our God is God of anything and everything.**

Jesus speaks to His disciples many times on this subject:

"*With man this is impossible, but with God all things are possible*" (Matthew 19:26 ESV).

"*For with God, nothing [is or ever] shall be impossible*" (Luke 1:37 AMP).

"*Humanly speaking, it is impossible. But not with God. Everything is possible with God*" (Mark 10:27). **Our God is God of the impossible!**

God's Vision is Perfect

The hospital that treated my cancer was a teaching hospital. I was asked many questions multiple times when the team would come into my room. One morning, a new doctor assessed my condition. Within the list of questions regarding my pain level, medical history, and symptoms, she asked, "Are you experiencing double vision?" I replied, "No, but I'd really like for you to introduce me to your twin."

It took just a beat for her to figure out it was a joke. I think Phil and I enjoyed that moment more than she or the rest of my "Grey's Anatomy" team did!

God's vision is perfect and far-seeing while ours is dim, distorted, and near-sighted. We only see the pain, the fear, the sadness, the ugliness, the evil, the loneliness. We see the current, the right now. God sees the comprehensive view, from beginning to end. He sees our complete story, and we can trust that the end of our story will be better than all the other chapters!

God is not the author of evil, but He can take it and weave it into a story better than we could have ever asked or imagined.

"Now to Him who is able to [carry out His purpose and] do superabundantly more than all that we dare ask or think [infinitely beyond our greatest prayers, hopes, or dreams], according to His power that is at work within us, to Him be the glory in the church and in Christ Jesus throughout all generations forever and ever. Amen" (Ephesians 3:20-21 AMP).

What an incredible promise! In Christ, God promises that He can and will use dark and difficult times for our good. *We can absolutely, certainly, without a shadow of a doubt, trust Him*!

CHAPTER 3

"Why ... Why ... Why ... Why?!"

Nancy Kerrigan

Our family loves vacationing at the beach. Any beach will do, but we especially love the Gulf Shores, Alabama area. In the summer of 2016, we rented a condo for a week and enjoyed the beautiful sights, sounds, smells, and rhythms of the sea. One late afternoon, I sat on the balcony, watching all the activity on the beach. There were kids on their skimmer boards, toddlers digging in the sand, young adults playing Frisbee, and out in the Gulf, just beyond the sand bar, was a pod of dolphins making an occasional appearance.

I also noticed some activity around the sea turtle nest that was just outside our condo. There was the well-known black netting around a small parcel of sand, and I saw a small group of people who seemed to be loitering a little too close to the netting. At first, I was perturbed by their insensitivity.

Then I noticed their matching green shirts, which indicated that they were conservationists. They seemed to have lots of knowledge concerning this particular part of the beach as I saw them point up the beach, down the beach, and then to this sea turtle nest. The longer I watched, the bigger the crowd of onlookers grew.

Slowly and carefully, the protective netting was dismantled, folded up, and put to the side, as ceremonially as someone taking down and folding up the American flag. Then two of the Green Shirts gently got down on their hands and knees and began stroking the sand slowly from side to side. Woman Green Shirt dragged the sand for a while, then sat back, her body language indicating that she didn't find what she had hoped for. The onlookers seemed to sigh.

Then Man Green Shirt (who seemed like the leader) began gently digging in the sand in another area. Now and then he would stop and say something to the onlookers. It looked like they weren't even breathing because of the anticipation.

All of the sudden, the crowd started clapping! They looked at the leader of the Green Shirts who must have been telling them something very interesting because they didn't take their eyes off him! I saw a few people start taking pictures of something in the sand. Then Head Green Shirt bent down and gently picked up what I realized was a baby sea turtle or "hatchling." (I just googled that.) He started walking toward the sea, and the crowd walked with him.

Wow! I always thought the babies crawled to the sea by themselves! I wished I had been down there to see that little hatchling and hear what Head Green Shirt was saying!

He carefully placed the baby turtle on the sand right at the water's edge, and I could just imagine the hushed awe that everyone in that small crowd felt. The waves were very gentle and took the turtle slowly out in the water. I could follow where the turtle was in the water by watching the crowd's faces. You could see everyone rooting for this little guy as he swam on top of the water.

By this time, several of my family members had joined me on the balcony to watch. I wondered out loud, "Do you think they named it?" It was fun and fascinating to watch.

I looked further out in the ocean to check on that pod of dolphins I had been watching. Could this day be any more perfect? A seagull caught my attention, and my eyes followed him as he dived down into the water. Suddenly, I heard a shriek and saw one of the turtle watchers point at the top of the water.

The seagull ate the turtle and flew away.

Boy, that crowd was *mad*.

Now, before I continue with this chapter, let me give you a chance to catch your breath. Just put the book down. Go ahead and grieve the early demise of the persistent little turtle. Have empathy toward the Green Shirts who were doing their best to preserve nature. Or you just might need to grab a box of tissues to wipe away the tears from laughing at the surprising turn of events. In any case, there will be no judgment. Just pick up the book when you are ready to continue.

Ready? Ok, let's continue. Now, I thought this entire event was beautiful … right up until the seagull ate the sea turtle. And then it turned downright hilarious! Not because I have a hidden disregard for sea turtles but because of how the crowd responded. When I said, "Boy, that crowd was mad," I meant they were *really mad*. They wanted to take down that seagull! They shouted at and shook their fists at it. Head Green Shirt took off his hat and threw it into the water in defeat, and one very valiant turtle watcher tried to chase down the bird. He picked up an inflated inner tube and hurled it at Sneaky Pete the Seagull while shouting words that I'm glad I didn't hear. At first, it seemed like Sneaky thought the man was chasing him to give him some food because he turned back toward the man for a moment. When he saw there was no bread flying into the air, though, he shrugged his shoulders and flew away.

Did they think they could scare the seagull into dropping the sea turtle? That the sea turtle would fall gracefully into their waiting hands, and they would put it out to sea again? And did they think that, being given a second chance at life, the sea turtle would defy the odds, make it out to sea, live for several years drifting with the currents (known as the "lost years"), and finally settle close to shore where it may take it more than 30 years to reach to adulthood? (I may or may not have done more research than needed on the life of the sea turtle.) Did they think if this sea turtle was female, that 30-50 years later, it would make its way back to the beach where it was born to lay its eggs? And if they happened to be on that beach at that exact time, would this sea turtle would give them a high-five with her flipper?

This was crazy!

The turtle watchers and the Green Shirts didn't seem to know what to do. They didn't even try to console each other. Finally, they began to disperse slowly. Beach activities continued, but because the sun was setting, it was thinning out on the beach. I wondered why Head Green Shirt didn't gather the other conservationists and turtle watchers together and say something like, "Well, I know it is sad, but this is what happens to the majority of hatchlings trying to make it into the water. We gave him a slight advantage by carrying him across the sand and out of the reach of crabs, birds, dogs, and feet, but once he was released into the water, he was essentially on his own. I'm sorry you had to see it, but the truth of the matter is that only 1 in 1,000 hatchlings survive to adulthood. Let's all celebrate that we got to have front row seats as we experienced the wonder of birth and the circle of life." I honestly thought since he had taken the time to teach them before he lifted Hank the Hatchling from his birth place and carried him to the sea, he would finish his lesson on birth and death, just like a good parent does with a child who loses a goldfish. But he didn't do it.

And then I saw Head Green Shirt. He was alone, sitting cross-legged at the edge of the water, his head in his hands in utter defeat. I watched him for a long time. He didn't move. No one came to sit beside him. The sun was setting; my balcony perch was getting cooler.

"Well, nothing more to see here," I thought, and I went inside.

Just kidding. I'm not finished. I do have a reason for this story. It really did happen exactly as I told it, and I can't help but draw some parallels to our own lives when we go through difficult times. From my birds-eye view of the situation, I can see myself in each of the characters in the story. There have been times when I was shocked at the things going on around me, and I just stood there stunned, like the onlookers, not knowing what to do next. There have been times when I've been angry and wanted to yell, scream, cry, or even throw something at the situation! And then there have been plenty of times when I've been so discouraged I just wanted to plop down, put my head in my hands, and wonder "Why?"

Have you been there? Are you there now?

Why is she pregnant and not me? She already has four kids and didn't want anymore, and here I've been praying for a child for six years!

Why did he get that promotion? I go to church every week, tithe faithfully, and he is perhaps the most ungodly man I've ever known!

Why did my wife get cancer? She doesn't deserve it! I do!

Why can't I catch a break? Am I always going to miss being in the right place at the right time?

Asking "why?" is a normal question when going through difficult times. Even Jesus cried out to His Father from the cross, *"My God, My God, why have you forsaken me?"* (Matthew 27:46 NIV). At the very moment that Jesus took all of humanity's sin on Himself, He felt abandoned. Now, He wasn't abandoned by God any more than we are when we face trials and difficulties, but He, being fully God and fully human, *felt* alone and deserted.

Just because we are believers and love God doesn't guarantee us an answer to all our questions. As a matter of fact, we are pretty much guaranteed that many of our questions *won't* be answered until we get to heaven.

> *"We don't yet see things clearly. We're squinting in a fog, peering through a mist. But it won't be long before the weather clears and the sun shines bright! We'll see it all then, see it all as clearly as God sees us, knowing him directly just as he knows us!" (1 Corinthians 13:12 MSG).*

In the meantime, what should we do while we are seeking the answers to our "why" questions? Paul goes on to tell us some great words:

> *"But for right now, until that completeness, we have three things to do to lead us toward that consummation: Trust steadily in God, hope unswervingly, love extravagantly. And the best of the three is love." (1 Corinthians 13:13 MSG).*

Trust Steadily in God

Did you know that God can be trusted even when He doesn't give you an answer? He is the one absolute in every trial and difficulty.

> *"Come to me, all of you who are weary and carry heavy burdens, and I will give you rest." (Matthew 11:28).*

> *"And be sure of this: I am with you always, even to the end of the age." (Matthew 28:20).*

> *"O Lord God of Heaven's Armies! Where is there anyone as mighty as you, O Lord? You are entirely faithful." (Psalm 89:8).*

"He will cover you with his feathers. He will shelter you with his wings. His faithful promises are your armor and protection." (Psalm 91:4).

"If we are unfaithful, he remains faithful, for he cannot deny who he is." (2 Timothy 2:13).

When you are tired and burdened, He can be trusted to give you rest. When you feel alone, He can be trusted to be with you. When you feel beaten, attacked, and betrayed, He can be trusted to shelter and protect you. When you have doubts and questions, He can be trusted to remain faithful and true to who He is.

As I walked through my cancer journey, I never asked, "Why me?". I was sad, and I cried some, especially when I thought I wouldn't have a chance to get to know my new granddaughter, Emma Jo. But I didn't cry out to God in anger or bitterness that I didn't deserve this diagnosis. I don't believe the bad things that happen to us, whether health crises, difficult financial situations, or tough relationship issues, are punishments from God. But I do believe that God uses these and other difficult things to bring us closer to Him.

Notice where David says God is in times of trouble: *"The Lord is close to the brokenhearted; he rescues those whose spirits are crushed."* (Psalm 34:18).

Pastor Rick Warren says, "Your most profound and intimate experiences of worship will likely be in your darkest days—when your heart is broken, when you feel abandoned, when you're out of options, when the pain is great—and you turn to God alone."[13]

During my treatment, I had to take some very strong medicines that made me talk in my sleep. I woke myself up many times by having passionate "conversations" about my jewelry business, my medical treatment, my daughter's upcoming wedding, or just breaking up a bowl of cornbread for Thanksgiving dressing. Phil was the silent eavesdropper on many of those conversations. Sometimes he heard them from beginning to end, and other times he walked into the room and asked me what I'd been doing. I'd say, "Well, I just led a whole group of ladies in New Jeweler Orientation, and I'm exhausted!"

One night I could hear myself talking to my doctors. Of course, I was dreaming, but even now I can see the room, and I can hear myself speaking fervently to the team of doctors gathered around my hospital bed. I said, "I want you to know how much I appreciate your help and advice in my treatment, and I know you are doing everything you can to treat this cancer. But I want you to know that my trust isn't in the treatment. My trust is in God, and whatever the outcome of all of this—whether I am healed or whether my time on earth is over—I know He will be glorified in it."

The next morning, Phil asked me if I remembered my dream. He repeated what I remembered, and he said that it was as if there really were doctors standing around my bed. My speech was not slurred from sleep or medicine but was direct and final. And when I finished, I went back to sleep.

How did I get that level of trust in God? It's certainly not because I am a spiritual giant! I have areas of failure, faithlessness, and doubt just like the next person. But I DO believe every word of the Bible, and from an early age, my parents taught me that God can be trusted no matter how difficult the circumstances or situation. Each time I faced a trial in my life, I brought it to the feet of Jesus. Step by step, trial after trial, difficulty upon difficulty, I trusted God. He didn't always provide answers, at least not to my liking, but He was always near me when I was broken-hearted. He protected me when I was afraid, and He was faithful to love and accept me even when I was unfaithful. I learned that He can be trusted.

When you have questions about something that breaks your heart, makes you afraid, or causes you to doubt that God cares, you can know for sure that He is near. Psalm 34:18 not only says that God is near to the brokenhearted, but this verse shows that it's not until your heart is broken and you are at the end of yourself that you are able to see that God is near you and has been there all the time.

Ask Him for specific Bible verses that are just for you. Write them down and post them around your house or in your car. Don't let the enemy have control over your thinking. Instead, use this time to build your trust in God even when you don't see His hand. You do not know what challenges might be ahead for you, and you'll need the level of trust that I had while going through cancer.

Hope Unswervingly

I'm an underdog cheerleader. I like rooting for the underdog, and I especially love the underdog stories of the Bible. Even though David was anointed as king when he was a young boy, he still had a lot to go through to get to that position. He writes about it in Psalms, and while he is never afraid to reveal his true feelings about disappointment, abandonment, and betrayal, he always finishes his songs with praise to God and a firm belief in His power and sovereignty.

Another one of my favorite underdogs in the Bible is Jeremiah. He was a prophet whom God called from a young age to speak to the nation of Israel. Known as the "Weeping Prophet," he was required by God to speak words of warning to a disobedient nation. Jeremiah cried many tears, not only because he knew what was about to happen but because no matter how hard he tried, the people would not listen. He had no human comfort since God had forbidden him to marry and have children. His friends turned their backs on him, and even though he preached for 40 years, he saw no real success in changing or softening the hearts of the people. He must have been very lonely and frustrated.

Jeremiah writes about this in Lamentations:

"He has made me chew on gravel. He has rolled me in the dust. Peace has been stripped away, and I have forgotten what prosperity is. I cry out, "My splendor is gone! Everything I had hoped for from the Lord is lost!" The thought of my suffering and homelessness is bitter beyond words. I will never forget this awful time, as I grieve over my loss." (Lamentations 3:16–20).

Have you ever been in a place like this? Have things ever been so bad that you say, "I will never forget this awful time!"?

For Jeremiah, in the midst of all his struggles, one small word changes everything: "Yet." Sometimes it's the smallest words in Scripture that matter the most. "Yet" tells us something can change. "Yet" tells us that the trials that keep coming can develop into something better. Jeremiah chooses to remember, and in making that choice, he finds hope. He says in verse 21, "Yet, I still dare to hope when I remember this." What does he remember? He decides to look at the truth of God and who God is. In the midst of a terrible trial, he makes a list that brings him hope:

1. "The steadfast love of the Lord NEVER CEASES!"

There aren't too many events, activities, or even commitments in this temporal world that we can stamp "Never Ends" on. Finances end, friendships end, marriages end, lives end. But God's faithful love *never* ends. He can be trusted to love you no matter what you've done or haven't done. He looks at you with a love and acceptance that can only dimly be compared with the love you feel for your children or your pets.

2. "His mercies NEVER COME TO AN END."

Mercies are plural because He pours out mercy after mercy after mercy. You will never be able to exhaust God's love and forgiveness no matter how many times you repeat an offense.

3. They are new EVERY MORNING."

Every day is a new day of hope with God. Each day that we see the sun rise, we have a day filled with God's love, forgiveness, compassion, goodness, and grace.

4. "Great is YOUR FAITHFULNESS."

Notice how Jeremiah gets so excited here that he talks directly to God! Just repeating that phrase of praise out loud can give you the perspective we all need to remember. We may be faithless or disappointing or hopeless, but God's faithfulness is GREAT. He never wavers, He never disappoints, and He always keeps His promises.

5. "The Lord is MY PORTION."

The word "portion" means inheritance. The Israelites had lost everything—their land, their homes, their jobs, and their temple—but God tells them not to worry about it! He will be their inheritance. What else could they need? And ultimately, what else do we need?

In the very center of your struggles, trials, and difficulties, take your eyes off your circumstances and stop asking "Why?". Instead say, "My hope is in God because His all-encompassing love for me never stops, He continually gives me mercy even when I don't deserve it. He offers me a new beginning every morning and is rooting for me to walk by His side. He has promised me an inheritance that is more beautiful and fulfilling than anything I can find on earth. Great is Your faithfulness, O God!"

Love Extravagantly

The Apostle Paul says that of these three—faith, hope, and love—love is the greatest (1 Corinthians 13:13). He tells us not just to love but to love *extravagantly*. If there is one thing that can help you take your eyes off your own difficult situation, it is to focus on others. When Phil and I first started walking through my health crisis, it would have been easy to focus only on us. It was several months and a couple of long hospital stays before we even had a diagnosis. We could have lived in panic and negativity, but while we were definitely afraid, we decided that our insecurity over the things we didn't understand could not be our focus.

Before my parents passed away, I was their primary caregiver. I loved how my parents would get to know the whole history of their nurses and caregivers in the hospital. My dad was especially good at this. When I visited, he would say, "Melody, this is Abu. He is from Tanzania and has been in America for 18 months." He would then tell me where Abu lived, how much schooling he had, whether or not he was married, and if he had kids. I couldn't believe how much information my dad was able to get! From the very beginning of my hospital stays, I decided that I was going to do the same thing. I was going to ask how I could pray for each one.

So, I did. When introduced to my nurses and techs, I would do my best to remember their names (their name tags were invariably turned around backward!). When we were alone, I would ask, "How can I pray for you?" They were almost always eager to tell me. I prayed for their kids to stay in school. I prayed for safety for their parents in their home country. I prayed for good grades in their graduate level classes. I prayed for their husbands to find good jobs. I prayed for them to find cheaper housing. Word began to get around, and sometimes I would have two or three techs in my room, just waiting for me to ask them, "How can I pray for you today?" I loved it!

The night before I was released from my three-week stay in rehab, I had a new tech. I had taken a few steps with the help of the parallel bars that afternoon, and Phil had captured it on video. I was excited, so I asked the tech if I could show her my progress. She shared my excitement and told me how proud she was. Then I asked, "How can I pray for you today?" She said, "Well, I would love for you to pray for my son. He is 11 and just had both his legs amputated from the knee down because of diabetes. Also, my husband just left us because he couldn't handle it."

Wow! Just before she shared her request, my tech was smiling and praising me and my accomplishment. If I had not asked her how I could pray for her, I doubt that she would have brought up her own story. You never know what another person is going through until you ask. I was completely honored to pray for her. We prayed and cried together.

Who can you pray for today? You don't have to look far; we see cries for help on social media every day. Press "like" and comment that you will be praying. Every "like" and every comment I received while battling CNS Lymphoma were so uplifting to me. I read them over and over.

Take your desire to love a step further by having note cards available so that you can send a handwritten message of hope and prayer. Record the names of the people you are praying for in a notebook or prayer journal. You don't have to set aside four hours a day to pray. Just look over the names and their requests for prayer. Call their names out to God. He knows how to answer.

Don't forget to bring your own anxieties to the Lord. I know many of you have heavy burdens. God never intended for you to carry those weights.

"Give all your worries and cares to God, for he cares about you." (1 Peter 5:7).

The word "give" (or "cast" in some translations) isn't a picture of us handing over our worries or tossing them at the feet of Jesus. In the original language, it is a picture of someone carrying a burden so heavy that all they can do is release it by opening their hands or dropping their arms. Right now, I pray you will loosen your grip on your questions and anxieties. You may have a burden so big that you aren't able to tell anyone about it. But God is big enough to carry that burden for you. Give your worries and cares to God. I pray that you will begin to live in the confidence that God is too good to do anything bad; that He is too wise to make a mistake; and that you would believe and trust Him no matter what.

Section Two

GOD
HEARS YOU

CHAPTER 4

"You talking to me?"

Taxi Driver

I'm what most nurses call "a hard stick." That just means that lab techs and nurses have a difficult time getting my blood drawn or finding a vein for an IV. My veins are deep, and they roll. Every two weeks I went to the hospital for treatment. I had a PICC line for my chemotherapy, but I had to have an IV for another drug that couldn't be administered the same way. Sometimes my nurses would get the vein with one try, and I couldn't even feel it; many times, it took several tries and sometimes two or even three different nurses. So, that was fun.

It was probably my third treatment in the hospital, and the nurse came in to start my IV. I remember particularly dreading the procedure. I smiled at my nurse and said, "I'm a hard stick. My veins are deep, and they roll." She looked at my arm and said, "Oh, I can see that!" At that moment, I got discouraged. I knew many people were praying for me and the side effects of my chemotherapy treatment, but I thought to myself, "I wish someone knew what is going on with me *right now.* I wish they knew that I am about to get stuck with a needle, possibly several times, and it is going to hurt!" I felt alone, but I knew I just had to take a deep breath and take it.

I smiled at my nurse and told her that I believed in her and was praying that she would get the IV on the first try. At that very moment, my phone alerted me to a Facebook private message. I didn't look to see who it was and thought it was probably someone inviting me to a group. Surprisingly and thankfully, my nurse did get the IV in on the first try, and I didn't even feel it! As soon as she left, I remembered the missed Facebook message. I picked up my phone and read this message from a friend across the country:

"Hi Melody, you crossed my mind this morning. I just wanted to let you know that we're thinking and praying for you. You've been such an encouragement to me and Kim. Jonathan"

"I will answer them before they even call to me. While they are still talking about their needs, I will go ahead and answer their prayers!" (Isaiah 65:24).

"When they call on me, I will answer; I will be with them in trouble. I will rescue and honor them." (Psalm 91:15).

God hears us when we call out to Him. He knows us so well that He has an answer even before we call! Let's think about that for a moment. The God of the universe, the all-knowing, all-powerful, creative force that made all things, who can be everywhere at once, is intimately aware of *us.* Let's bring it closer to home. He is intimately aware of *you.* God does not just know you exist. He is intimately in tune with you. When this thought hits David in Psalm 8, it blows his mind!

"When I look at the night sky and see the work of your fingers—the moon and the stars you set in place—what are mere mortals that you should think about them, human beings that you should care for them?" (Psalm 8:3–4).

Imagine David looking up at the night sky, being overwhelmed by the expanse of it and contemplating this fact. "It is incomprehensible that You would know me, that You would care for me, that You would listen to me, that You would be aware of me, and that you would want a relationship with me!"

God Initiates Prayer With Us

A few days before the official diagnosis, my doctor was convinced I had cancer. We had been fighting for an answer a little over a year. I had been in the hospital three different times (28 days total), and when I was at home, the pain forced me to retreat from all normal activity for weeks at a time. One week before our daughter's wedding, all the medicine quit working. The pain flooded in stronger than ever, and I had to be admitted once again to the hospital. Thankfully, I convinced them to release me the day of the wedding, but I was back in the hospital the very next day.

Once the doctors knew what they were looking for, my treatment plan worked like this:

1) Two weeks in the hospital for pain management, extensive testing, and a four-hour biopsy of the tumor in my spine
2) Another two weeks in the hospital for recovery and hospital-rehab
3) Three weeks in a rehab facility

After all this and a couple of weeks at home, my chemotherapy finally started. Because it was such a strong treatment, the chemotherapy had to be administered in the hospital. I stayed for 8-10 days and then went home for two weeks. And repeat. And repeat. And repeat.

I repeated the chemo-hospital-home cycle eight times. Whew! I tell you all of this because during these cycles, I got to know many nurses and techs. I loved them all! What an incredible opportunity to pray with as many as I could. My hospital room ended up being a happy place, and many of the nurses would step into my room just before going off-shift, smile at me, and say, "I've already put in my request to be your nurse when you come back." I liked it, not only because it was a compliment to me, but it kept me from retreating into myself and my own problems.

One afternoon, a nurse came by to tell me that she was leaving for the day and would be off the rest of my time in the hospital. She said she would see me when I checked back in the next time. At that very moment, it seemed like every medical professional in the hospital was standing around my bed—taking my statistics, changing my IV bags, bringing in my meal, introducing me to my tech and nurse for the next shift, and asking when I had my last BM. (If I was ever tempted to lie, it was in answering that last question because of the joy or disappointment my answer would bring. I'm kind of a people-pleaser. Sometimes, they weren't pleased.)

While I usually asked if I could pray with someone when it was just the two of us in the room, I felt like it was very important to ask this nurse how I could pray for her. I sat up as best I could in the bed, ignored all the activity around me, reached out for her hand, and said, "I haven't had a chance to ask you, but how can I pray for you this week?" She was pleasantly surprised, and she paused as she began to think. She said, "No one has ever asked me that before … I don't know what to say." I replied, "Sometimes it's hard to think of something on the spur of the moment, right?" She nodded her head. I said, "Well, just know that I will be praying for you while you are off work. Is that okay?" She said she thought that would be great, and we said goodbye until next time.

It was about three weeks before I saw her again, but the next time she was my nurse, she came in my room, and we talked for a while. Before leaving to go check on her other patients, she said, "I've been meaning to tell you. Do you remember saying that you would pray for me the last time I was your nurse?" I said that I did. She said, "Well, I went home that night, and I'm single, and there is no one to greet me except my cat that I've had for many years. When I walked in that night, I noticed that my cat had died while I was at work. I know it is silly, but I was very sad, and I suddenly felt very lonely. But then I remembered that you were praying for me! And even though I couldn't tell you how to pray, it comforted me just to know that you cared and you were praying."

God was the initiator of that prayer. When we face a dark moment, whether a crisis, a fear, a loneliness, or a sadness, and suddenly feel the need to pray for strength, our longing for help begins in the heart of God. Our desire to pray is the result of God's greater desire to have a relationship with us. He wants to talk with us, and He invites us to be an integral part of His plan.

The thought that God wants to work in me to accomplish His plans amazes me. I feel like David in Psalms: "Who am I in this enormous world that You would hear my cry? That you would want to be my friend? That You would invite me to experience You in a personal way and answer my requests as readily as my earthly father answers me?"

While my Facebook friend, Jonathan, didn't know I needed prayer at the moment of my IV, God knew. He brought my name to Jonathan's mind and told him to pray for me and message me that he was praying. When I called out to God for someone to be thinking about me, He already had the answer to my prayer!

Even though I didn't know my nurse would need prayer when she got home from work and found her cat had passed away, God knew. He put it in my heart to pray for her and to tell her that I would be praying for her even before she knew she would need it.

"It shall come to pass that before they call, I will answer; And while they are still speaking, I will hear" (Isaiah 65:24 NKJV).

God wants to hear our prayers so much that He prepares an answer before we even call! His greatest desire is for us to come to Him and present our requests. He hears us.

God Invites Us to Pray

Let's look at a verse in Jeremiah that many have said is God's cell phone number.

*"**Call to me** and I will answer you. I'll tell you marvelous and wondrous things that you could never figure out on your own" (Jeremiah 33:2–3 MSG).*

We are invited by God to call Him! I recently decided to allow God to direct my morning prayer time. I always follow a reading plan from my Bible app (YouVersion), but my prayer journal is typically about my needs and desires. I decided that my first prayer before I got out of bed would now be, "Lord, who do You want me to pray for today?" From the first day I started this habit, God has never failed to give me a name. Sometimes I get a text from a girlfriend needing prayer for one of her relatives. Sometimes I see a Facebook post from a friend requesting prayer over a difficult situation in her life or for a medical procedure she is facing that day. Other times the name of someone I haven't thought of in a while comes to my mind. I always write their name in my prayer journal, and I pray for them throughout the day. As many times as I can, I write the person a personal note of encouragement, or I text them a quick sentence of my thoughts or prayers for them. I can't tell you how many times I have received a phone call or a text from one of these people saying how my note or message came to them at just the right time.

God invites me to pray because He already has an answer He wants to give. He continues inviting me to pray because He wants a relationship with me. He invites me to pray because He loves me, and He wants to hear my voice.

Years ago, we were preparing for the birthday of our youngest son (Phillip). He always had a hard time trying to figure out what he wanted. Finally, he said he might like a bike, but he wasn't sure yet; he was still thinking. At the time, we knew we couldn't afford a brand-new bike, but we found a guy who refurbished bikes. We purchased one and hid it in the basement. Now, our task was to get Phillip to want a bike.

In the days leading up to his birthday, Phil and I talked a lot about bikes in front of him. We talked about how much fun it was to jump on our bikes and ride around the neighborhood with our friends and how much we enjoyed decorating our bikes with different accessories. The next time we asked what Phillip wanted for his birthday, he confidently answered, "I want a bike."

Our next question was, "What color do you want your bike to be?" He said, "Red." Of course he wanted a red bike. Red was his favorite color. But the bike we had stored in the basement was blue. Phil and I started talking to each other in front of Phillip about red bikes versus blue bikes.

Phil: *Red bikes are great. But doesn't it seem like everyone has a red bike?*
Me: *I do see a lot of red bikes.*
Phil: *You know what would be really cool? A blue bike!*
Me: *Oh yeah, a blue bike!*
Phil: *Would you want us to look for a blue bike for you, Phillip?*
Phillip: *No, I want a red bike.*

It took more than one conversation about the joy and beauty of a blue bike, but soon Phillip came around and informed us that if we were going to give him a bike for his birthday, he wanted it to be blue. So, on his birthday, we were able to give him exactly what he asked for—a beautiful blue bike! Isn't that the wish of every parent: to be able to give their child exactly what he or she wants?

This is an awesome picture of how God invites us to pray. He has gifts ready and waiting for us. He plants the desire in our hearts for the gifts He has prepared. Then we take the next step and pray for these desires to be met. Because He loves us and hears us, God is more than delighted to give us our requests. And since God's gifts are always the best, we can trust that they are exactly what we need.

God Ensures Us He Will Answer

Not only does God invite us to pray, but He also ensures us that He will answer.

> *"Call to me and I will answer you. I'll tell you marvelous and wondrous things that you could never figure out on your own"* (Jeremiah 33:2–3 MSG).

I know this has happened to you before. You are having a conversation with someone in the adjacent room. Maybe you are in the kitchen preparing a meal, and your husband is in the den folding clothes. The conversation is going well even though you don't see each other. After a short pause, you start talking again, this time with a long story about something that happened at work. You find yourself laughing as you describe the unexpected turn of events, and you can't wait to get his reaction so you can laugh together at this hilarious situation. You ask, "Can you believe that?" There is no answer from the other room. You say, "Honey?" Still no answer. You walk around the corner, and at the same time, you see your husband coming back into the room. He was out of the room during that whole story, putting away laundry and not hearing a word you said!

God is never out of the room. He is never out of earshot. He is never too busy, and He is never preoccupied. He is never uninterested. God hears us when we pray, and we can trust He will answer. This truth is seen over and over in the Bible.

*"Listen closely to my prayer, O Lord; hear my urgent cry. I will call to you whenever I'm in trouble, and **you will answer me.**" (Psalm 86:7).*

*"When they call on me, **I will answer**; I will be with them in trouble. I will rescue and honor them." (Psalm 91:15).*

*"I took my troubles to the Lord; I cried out to him, and **he answered my prayer.**" (Psalm 120:1).*

*"Then when you call, **the Lord will answer**. "Yes, I am here," **he will quickly reply.**" (Isaiah 58:9).*

*"For I am the Lord their God and **I will answer them.**" (Zechariah 10:6 ESV).*

*"For your Father knows exactly what you need **even before you ask** him!" (Matthew 6:8).*

*"Keep on asking, and you **will receive** what you ask for. Keep on seeking, and you will find. Keep on knocking, and the door will be opened to you. For everyone who asks, **receives**. Everyone who seeks finds. And to everyone who knocks, the door will be opened" (Matthew 7:7–8).*

Would you believe it if I said that God has already prepared an answer to your prayer, and He is just waiting for you to call on Him before He sends the answer? That is exactly what the above Scriptures are saying. God hears you, and He will answer you. When you call on Him in prayer, it draws you closer to Him. When He answers, it deepens your faith and teaches you that He can be trusted. God delights in your prayers in the same way a parent delights in being able to give their children what they ask for.

You may say, "I pray, but He never answers." I understand. There have been times I've felt the same way. But if we believe that every word of the Bible is true, then we must believe that every time we pray, He answers.

Maybe you need to ask yourself a couple of questions: Are you praying, or are you just thinking about praying? Are you praying, or are you worrying? Are you praying or just talking it over with a friend? Are you praying or just wishing? Are you praying, or are you trying to figure it out on your own? We may do any number of things, including telling others that we are praying about it, but we've actually never brought it to the One who matters most.

Prayer isn't about a posture, a place, or a pattern. *It is simply a conversation with God.* It can be silent or audible. It can be in your favorite chair at home, on your knees at church, or in your car driving to work. The only requirement is that it must be real—as real as a conversation with a friend over coffee.

"Don't worry about anything; instead, pray about everything. Tell God what you need, and thank him for all he has done. Then you will experience God's peace, which exceeds anything we can understand. His peace will guard your hearts and minds as you live in Christ Jesus." (Philippians 4:6–7).

When you bring your requests, concerns, and questions to God, He can be trusted to answer. It may not be the answer you are looking for. It may not be the timing you are hoping for. It may not the way you are planning for it to happen. But He will answer! And when He answers, you can be sure that it is exactly what you need.

"So let us come boldly to the throne of our gracious God. There we will receive his mercy, and we will find grace to help us when we need it most." (Hebrews 4:16).

God Illuminates His Plan for Our Lives

*"Call to me and I will answer you. **I'll tell you marvelous and wondrous things that you could never figure out on your own.**" (Jeremiah 33:2–3 MSG).*

Not only are we invited to call to God and not only has He promised to answer us, but He also says that when we pray, He will talk to us about the marvelous and wondrous things He has planned for us. Isn't that exciting? Wouldn't you like to have the kind of relationship with God that when you call out to Him, He not only answers, but He also plants in your heart "marvelous and wonderful things" that are going to happen?

Even if you are a skeptic, what would it hurt for you to try it? Go ahead. Imagine yourself walking into the throne room of God to make a request that you would not be embarrassed to ask for. Not something from selfish motives ("I would like a million dollars.") Not a demand or an ultimatum. ("If you give me that promotion that I'm not even in line for, then I'll go to church.") Not an instruction of how you expect God to work. ("I know You told us to take that job in Omaha, but You need to bring a buyer for our house first, and then we'll do it.")

Just pray. Talk to Him.

Ask God to give your husband a group of godly men to support his desire to lead your family and walk in purity.

Pray about your honest feelings regarding your circumstances (fear, anxiety, anger, depression, hopelessness).

Ask God for wisdom and discernment when you have a difficult decision to make.

Pray about being a better parent.

Pray about learning how to love a family member who talks about you behind your back.

Pray about anything and everything. God wants to hear it all. And when you start having daily, even hourly, conversations with Him, God says He will illuminate your path by telling you great and mighty things.

> *"Oh, how great are God's riches and wisdom and knowledge! How impossible it is for us to understand his decisions and his ways! For who can know the Lord's thoughts? Who knows enough to give him advice? And who has given him so much that he needs to pay it back? For everything comes from him and exists by his power and is intended for his glory. All glory to him forever! Amen" (Romans 11:33–36).*

> *"Have you ever come on anything quite like this extravagant generosity of God, this deep, deep wisdom? It's way over our heads. We'll never figure it out. Is there anyone around who can explain God? Anyone smart enough to tell him what to do? Anyone who has done him such a huge favor that God has to ask his advice? Everything comes from him; Everything happens through him; Everything ends up in him. Always glory! Always praise! Yes. Yes. Yes." (Romans 11:33–36 MSG).*

What great and mighty things, what marvelous and wondrous things does God have planned for you? I don't know what He has for you, but when you start spending time with God in prayer, you can know. It doesn't take hours a day in prayer, but it does require consistency. It doesn't require enormous faith to start praying and asking God to reveal Himself and His plan to you. It just requires faith the size of a mustard seed.

Jesus talks about this in the book of Mark. He is telling a story about a mustard seed—the smallest seed known at that time. He is trying to describe to the people what a kingdom life looks like. He wants them to see the great and mighty things God has in store for those that believe. He says,

> *"What shall we say the kingdom of God is like, or what parable shall we use to describe it? It is like a mustard seed, which is the smallest of all seeds on earth. Yet when planted, it grows and becomes the largest of all garden plants, with such big branches that the birds can perch in its shade." (Mark 4:30–32 NIV).*

The phrase that sticks out to me is "Yet when planted, it grows." That is how God works throughout history. He accepts us just the way we are. When we step out and plant the smallest amount of faith, it grows.

What does this look like? It looks like a woman struggling to write words for a book that will impact people. It looks like an old man trying to start a new ministry. It looks like a young couple moving to Detroit to start something from nothing. Yet when planted, faith grows.

It looks like a wife who has prayed for her husband to come to Christ for 30 years. It looks like parents who are struggling to help with tough love a child addicted to drugs. It looks like a single mom who works two jobs so she can keep her kids in a Christian school. Yet when planted, faith grows.

You may only have faith the size of a mustard seed, but if you just hold onto that seed—protecting it, preserving it, picturing it—nothing will change. If you want to see great and mighty things happen in your life, you must take the first step and plant that seed. Even in the soil of skepticism, doubt, and adversity, that seed will grow.

Trust that God will illuminate the plan He has for you. It's a good plan, even if you are in a dark moment. Let Him show you how He can get good out of bad.

CHAPTER 5

"Do you understand the words that are coming out of my mouth?"

Rush Hour

When my sister's boys were little, she struggled with the same thing that most parents do—wondering if what she said was getting through to them! As her three boys piled into the car after school one afternoon, my sister leaned very close to her oldest son's face and started fussing at him for not cleaning his room before school like he said he would. As she was emphatically "training him up in the way he should go," she noticed that his eyes never left her face. He was intently staring at her. She thought to herself, "Well, finally! I think I'm really getting through to him. What a great mom-moment I am having!" Since she had his complete attention, she leaned in a little closer and continued her instruction a little longer. And then to punctuate her parental pedagogy, she said, "Christopher, do you understand what I am saying?" After a short pause, Christopher said, "You sure have big teeth."

Fix Your Focus

When you are going through a dark time, it can be extremely difficult to focus on the promises of God, especially when all you can see are the "big teeth" of disappointment or discouragement. Sometimes the hot breath of fear and anger threaten to take away the truth of God's word—that He can be trusted, that He is faithful, and that He is good. When focus is hard, trust is hard.

For me, the physical pain was sometimes so intense that all I could do was close my eyes and pray for sleep. When sleep wouldn't come, I knew I could read my Bible for comfort or pick up one of the many devotional books my sweet friends and family sent me. But in all honesty, I found I couldn't concentrate long enough to allow those words to sink in and comfort me. In those moments, I was grateful for the short phrases of encouragement and truth that I had stored in my heart from childhood. "The Lord is my Shepherd." "Do not fear for I am with you." "I know the plans I have for you." "Taste and see that the Lord is good." "Nothing can separate us from the love of God." "Great is your faithfulness." "Everything is possible with God." "When I am afraid, I will put my trust in You."

Even though I couldn't quote the chapter and verse, these promises reminded me of God's love for me. And in pain, that's about all I could concentrate on. God welcomes that kind of conversation with Him. He knows we are "but dust" (Psalm 103:14 NASB), so He sent the Holy Spirit to interpret even our groaning to God.

"Meanwhile, the moment we get tired in the waiting, God's Spirit is right alongside helping us along. If we don't know

how or what to pray, it doesn't matter. He does our praying in and for us, making prayer out of wordless sighs, our aching groans." (Romans 8:26 MSG).

Have you ever found yourself in such a dark time that all you could do was throw yourself on your bed and just cry? You tried to pray, but all you could get out was "Oh, God." That's ok! He gave us the Holy Spirit to take our words and make sense out of them! The very best thing you can do in your dark moment is to turn your focus to God. My mom always told me that we tend to focus on our problems and only occasionally take those problems to God in prayer. She said we should practice the exact opposite in our lives: Keep our glance on our problems and our gaze on our God. He can handle it. When we focus on Him, we can trust that He hears us and cares for us.

How do we keep our focus on God? Paul tells us what to do in his letter to the Philippians:

"Don't worry about <u>anything</u>; instead, pray about <u>everything</u>. Tell God what you need, and thank him for <u>all</u> he has done. Then you will experience God's peace, which exceeds <u>anything</u> we can understand." (Philippians 4:6–7, underlining mine).

The words I underlined are called indefinite pronouns. They are used to refer to nonspecific persons or things. There is no beginning or ending to these words; they are all-encompassing.

I believe this is what we think the verse says:

"Don't worry about the <u>bad things</u> that are happening in your life. Pray only about the <u>difficult or unexplainable things</u>. Tell God a <u>few big things</u> you need, and thank Him for <u>only the good things</u> He has done. Then you will experience God's peace, which exceeds <u>a few things</u> we can understand."

My version of that verse isn't that bad. It's good. It's a start. But it's not the best! God always has something better for us.

Paul tells us not to worry about anything—good or bad. He tells us to pray about everything—good and bad. We are to talk to God about all we need—big and small. We are to thank Him in all things—good and bad. Then we will experience God's peace which goes beyond anything, in this world or the next, we can understand.

Wow! That's a pretty big revelation! Can you even imagine a life where you didn't worry about anything at all? Where you prayed about everything and had a thankful attitude in everything? And can you even imagine living in the peace of God that goes beyond anything you can understand? That sounds like heaven to me. But we don't have to wait for heaven. This is the relationship God has for us right now.

The next logical question you may have is, "But, how?" It goes back to your focus. When you allow your mind to circle constantly around your fears and worries, your focus is on your problems, and your glance is on God. Stop torturing yourself with the thoughts, "Why did he leave me?" "Why did she die?" "Why is this prayer never answered?" "Why did I lose my job?" "Why did I get cancer?" "Why did she betray me?" You think that if you can figure it out, solve it, or prepare for it, you can keep it from happening again.

But the truth is that until we reach the other side, until we are in heaven, there will be pain. What you really need when you are in the darkest times is not answers for your pain but presence through your pain. In your deepest pain, you don't need explanations; you need God. An explanation doesn't take away the hurt. But God's presence—the promise that He hasn't left you and you are not alone—comforts you in your pain.

"Behold, I am with you and will keep [careful watch over you and guard you] wherever you may go ... for I will not leave you until I have done what I have promised you." (Genesis 28:15 AMP).

*"For He has said, "I WILL NEVER [under any circumstances]
DESERT YOU [nor give you up nor leave you without sup-
port, nor will I in any degree leave you helpless], NOR WILL
I FORSAKE or LET YOU DOWN or RELAX MY HOLD
ON YOU [assuredly not]!" (Hebrews 13:5 AMP).*

*"This is my command—be strong and courageous! Do not
be afraid or discouraged. For the Lord your God is with you
wherever you go." (Joshua 1:9).*

The minute you recognize that you are circling the drain
with worry, turn your focus on His Word and the promises
like these. He can be trusted; He has not deserted you, and
He will not leave you—ever.

Remember God's Faithfulness

Many of you know that the heavy medication received after
surgery can play with your mind. There were lots of times
I did and said things that were quite comical to the people
observing me. After one of my four-hour long MRI's, my friend
Elizabeth, texted me to see how I was doing. She knew I was
very claustrophobic and wanted to know if this time was any
easier with the stronger drugs the hospital gave me. Here is
what I texted her in my drugged induced state:

*"Well, I made it through. Was it easy? Was it comfortable? Was I
in my happy place where joy is transcendent and serene dreams
comfort me in quiet bliss? No. I felt like a sweet baby puppy
stuffed inside a panty hose and then shoved into a PVC pipe until
my torturers were bored with the experience and let me out".*

My daughter, Mary, remembers another time when I
was babbling on about my family to my nurse and the other
attendants taking me back to my room. (I always seemed to
be quite talkative when coming out from under the influence

of the medication.) Mary said I was telling them all about my kids and my husband and that they would be waiting for me in my room. I said my mom and dad would be there and my mother and father-in-law, too. (I thought I was dreaming that I was telling them these things, but I guess I was talking in my sleep again!) The next thing I remember was the stunned look on my nurse's face. I remember thinking, "Uh oh. I wonder what I just said." Apparently, I completed my story with a very blunt, "No wait. They're dead." I guess I had a moment of clarity and decided it was important to let them know that my parents and in-laws would not, in fact, be in the room because they were no longer with us.

When we first started noticing the symptoms of the disease, Mary became my driver and, many times, my patient advocate. I couldn't always remember all the things the different doctors told me, and she was right there by my side listening so that we could tell Phil exactly what was going on. At each new doctor's office, there was new paperwork to complete. One time just for fun, as I was filling out more forms, I asked, "Mary, have I ever had brain surgery?" Never looking up from her magazine, she answered, "No. It's on your bucket list." That still makes me laugh.

What do these stories have to do with remembering God's faithfulness? I'll get to that part, but mostly I just wanted to tell you some funny things that happened along the way. I wish I could remember everything because we laughed a lot. Laughter is a great way to get through the dark moments of your life.

What makes people laugh? Did you know that as far back as Aristotle, philosophers have debated this question and have even written books about it? Sigmund Freud wrote an essay entitled "Jokes and their Relation to the Unconscious." A real side-splitter, I'm sure. In all the theories, two elements seem to be present when making something funny: contradiction and surprise. Both elements capitalize on the twist and the

59

unexpected—something that doesn't make sense or something you didn't see coming. It's what lies behind the humor of a one-liner like "I like to hold hands at the movies ... which always seems to startle strangers."

God allowed laughter to come into the lives of people all through the Bible to help them get through difficult days. The story in Genesis 18 and 21 of the impossible birth of Isaac to a 100-year-old man and a 90-year-old woman has both elements of contradiction and surprise. It made Sarah LOL when she overheard God tell Abraham, "About this time next year ... your wife, Sarah, will have a son!" (Genesis 18:10).

I imagine that God set the joke up something like this:

God: *Hey Abraham, do you remember when I changed your name from Abram ("Father of Many") to Abraham ("Father of a Multitude"), and even though you didn't have any kids, you told everyone to call you by your new name?*

Abraham: *Yep. The gang sure got a kick out of that. It took a few years for some of them to be able to say my name without snickering.*

God: *And remember when I renamed Sarah and told her that she would give birth to nations and kings?*

Abraham: *Yes, I do, and 24 years later, Sarah still thinks that's a hoot.*

God: *Ok. Where is Sarah?*

Abraham: *She is in the tent.*

God: *Awesome! I can't wait to see her face when I tell her that this time next year, she is going to have a son! She is going to laugh her head off!*

In the doorway of the tent, Sarah overhears the joke and totally misses the punchline. She laughs, but she doesn't think it's funny "HaHa", more like "Does this milk taste funny?"

She laughs the laugh of a cynic. The laugh of someone who has lost hope. Her long time of waiting has taken away her sense of humor. While she laughs at the preposterousness of this prediction—an old woman with one foot in the grave and the other in the maternity ward—she expects no surprises from God.

God says to Abraham, "Why did Sarah laugh?" Sarah quickly moves back into the darkness of the tent and says under her breath, "I didn't laugh." And God says, without even looking in her direction, "Yes you did; you laughed."

I can imagine that Sarah with her hands over her ears after she was called out by God for laughing, saying to herself, "No, no! Don't stir this up again! I gave up my hope of having a child a long time ago. It's ridiculous now, and I won't go through this again." She might not have even heard Him ask, "Is anything too hard for God?" If she could have heard that question, and if she could have answered "No, there is nothing too hard for God," contradiction and surprise would have come together, and she would have been able to throw her head back and laugh as she had never laughed before. Probably laughing and crying at the same time.

To get through any dark or difficult moment in our lives, we cannot forget God's faithfulness. God is faithful no matter how long we wait, no matter how bleak the situation, no matter what others think or say, no matter how impossible it seems. God keeps His promises, and He is faithful.

> "The faithful love of the Lord never ends! His mercies never cease. Great is his faithfulness; his mercies begin afresh each morning. I say to myself, 'The Lord is my inheritance; therefore I will hope in him!'" (Lamentations 3:22–23).

Sarah laughs twice in this story in Genesis. Her first laugh is the laugh of the cynic, but her second laugh is a laugh of gratefulness and joy. God does what He promised. Abraham and Sarah DO have a son, and they name him Isaac, which means "He laughs." Sarah says *"God has brought me laughter. All who hear about this will laugh with me"* (Genesis 21:6).

I can just imagine that every time Abraham or Sarah called Isaac in for dinner, they smiled at each other and couldn't help but giggle about how God used their lives to demonstrate His faithfulness to His Word in such a hilarious and surprising way. They never forgot His faithful love in their lives.

> *"The Lord will work out his plans for my life—for your faithful love, O Lord, endures forever." (Psalm 138:8).*

> *"The Lord will fulfill his purpose for me; your steadfast love, O Lord, endures forever." (Psalm 138:8 ESV).*

Fix your focus on God and His purposes for your life. He is faithful to complete His plans for you—always.

Pray Fearlessly

Our oldest son, Paul, had a job a few years ago as a landscape engineer for our school district. One afternoon, he and another engineer went to grade the playground of an elementary school because it had some standing water. While the other engineer waited with the equipment, Paul walked onto the playground to survey the damage and see where they would start the repair. It was recess, and as he walked toward the building, he saw a small group of boys huddled together, pointing at him and talking about him. As he got closer, he heard them saying to each other, "You ask him." "No, you ask!" "No look, he's right there, you ask him!" Paul wasn't allowed to talk to the kids, so he just kept walking. When he turned around and had to walk past them again, they had gathered a few more boys and were saying the same things—"There he is! Go over and ask him!" "He's coming right by us. Just go over and ask!"

Paul asked the other engineer if he knew what the kids wanted, but he didn't know any more than Paul. They couldn't begin their work until all the kids left the playground, so they just waited by their equipment and kept watching this curious event unfold. It wasn't long before the group of three or four boys turned into a gang of nine or ten, and soon they were all fist pumping and chanting a four-word phrase in unison. Paul and the other engineer still couldn't hear what the kids were chanting, but it was obvious the chant was aimed at them!

They watched as more and more kids joined in the fist-pumping chant, and when the group got bigger and louder, their young, high-pitched voices could clearly be heard: "Dig us a hole! Dig us a hole! Dig us a hole!"

Paul and the other engineer … OK. I'm tired of writing "the other engineer" for the other character in this story, so let's call him "Barney." Paul and Barney suddenly realized that these boys saw them as the answer to an awesome request. They wanted a hole! What could be more fun for elementary school boys than to have a hole right in the middle of their playground?! The kids saw the equipment and two strong guys, and the chant couldn't help but come out. "Dig us a hole! Dig us a hole! Dig us a hole!"

In the middle of all the chanting, the teachers raised their hands to indicate it was time to line up and go inside. The boys lined up, but the chanting did not stop. As a matter of fact, it became contagious, and now all the kids were standing in line, jumping up and down, fist pumping, and chanting, "Dig us a hole! Dig us a hole! Dig us a hole!" Paul was certain that half the kids didn't even know why they were chanting, but peer allegiance drove the chant.

For some reason, the teachers did not stop the chant. It was near the end of the school day, and maybe they were just too tired to notice or care. Besides, since the kids were all committed to this one request, they weren't pushing or arguing among themselves. As the doors to the school opened, the organized lines of kids marched into the halls with this singular and definitive phrase: "Dig us a hole!" "Dig us a hole!" "Dig us a hole!"

Paul and Barney couldn't help but laugh. And as Paul told me the story, I couldn't help but laugh. Paul said it became one of the best experiences of his life!

As I had Paul repeat this story to different family members who hadn't heard it the first time, I began to wonder what made those boys think that Paul and Barney would dig them a hole? (I had no idea what "grading the school yard" meant, and I was picturing them leaning against two heavy duty shovels.) I asked Paul, "What in the world would make those kids think that two guys with shovels standing on their playground would dig them a hole?" He said, "Mom. We rolled up on the playground on a giant John Deere tractor." And at that moment, I understood. It was the tractor that gave those boys the hope that something exciting could happen. The boys saw the tractor and said to each other, "What could that tractor do? Well, a tractor could ... DIG US A HOLE! That would be awesome!!" And they realized that if there was ever a time to ask for a hole to be dug, this was the time!

I think we sometimes forget how big, how great, and how awesome God is. We think God has a shovel when He really has a tractor. As adults, we aren't bold enough for the big ask. When children pray, they aren't afraid of asking for anything. They have no problem believing that God is big enough to answer any request and handle anything brought before Him. In Matthew 18, Jesus teaches that we are to come to God like children. To come to God like a child is to expect awe-inspiring greatness.

When Phil pastored a church in Michigan, our children usually sat on the front row. One evening during Phil's sermon, our youngest son, Phillip, must have been fully engrossed in the message. When Phil posed a rhetorical question ("Is God the type of God who would leave you like that?"), five-year-old Phillip emphatically shouted out, "NO!"

Children have the ability to believe without complication, to have faith that moves mountains, and to embrace God's Word in all its simplicity. Your heavenly Father wants you to have this type of trust in Him. After all, you are His child. And He can be trusted to hear you in your dark moment.

One of my many favorite Scriptures of comfort and encouragement is Ephesians 3:20. Let's look at it word by word to see if it reveals something about God or something about yourself that you hadn't noticed before.

"Now all glory to God, who is able, through his mighty power at work within us, to accomplish infinitely more than we might ask or think."

Now: at this present moment, in this present circumstance
All: entire, complete, full, total, perfect
Glory to God: honor, majesty, prestige, triumph, splendor, praise
Who is Able: continues to be powerful, worthy, effortless, equipped, expert
Through: because of, by means of
His Mighty: robust, sturdy, strong, omnipotent
Power: skill, talent, influence
At work: in force, streaming, operating, rushing
Within: inside, inserted, in the midst of
Us: everyone
To accomplish: achieve, bring about, realize, produce
Infinitely: boundlessly, abundantly, enormously, immeasurably, extravagantly
More than: beyond, on top of, over and above
We: everyone
Might: be capable of
Ask: appeal, petition, request
Or think: imagine, visualize, conceive

Here is my personalization: "Right now, in this exact moment, whether it's a season of darkness or blessing, I give full and total glory and majesty to God because He is and always will be able, through His omnipotent power streaming within me, to bring about abundantly, enormously, and extravagantly beyond what I could ask for or even conceive of."

"God can do anything, you know—far more than you could ever imagine or guess or request in your wildest dreams!" (Ephesians 3:20 MSG).

Fix your focus, remember His faithfulness, and pray fearlessly! God is able. He is not only able to handle our biggest requests and go exceedingly above and beyond those requests; He is also able to handle our deepest wounds, our dirtiest secrets, and our darkest pits. There is absolutely nothing too big, too embarrassing, too shocking, or too unforgivable for God not to hear and love you through it.

CHAPTER 6

"What we have here is a failure to communicate."

Cool Hand Luke

It's writing day. I have my coffee on the TV tray, my computer on my lap, my cell phone on the sofa's armrest. Our sofa has a built-in footrest, so my feet are up. Our dogs are getting older, so they will either sleep on the floor near my feet or on either side of me with their heads on my shoulders. Our stage in life is known as the "empty-nester," so the house is quiet. Very quiet.

My fingers are positioned perfectly on my keyboard, hovering above the keys, waiting for inspiration. I re-read each sentence I've written, weighing each word, editing for precise clarity. I resist the urge to reach for the backspace button, erasing everything I've just written, starting over in a different direction. (And I'm wondering how long I can keep this going—writing about my writing process in the perfect symmetry found in these two paragraphs without actually writing about anything in particular.)

Then it happens. The air conditioner clicks off. I hadn't even noticed that it was running, but now that it is off, the house is really quiet. I can hear everything—the clock ticking in the dining room, the refrigerator running in the kitchen, cars driving by out front, a bird whistling in the backyard. What I thought was silence wasn't silence at all.

The minute the air conditioner stopped, I breathed a sigh of relief. My body said, "Ahhhhh." The continual background noise must have keyed me up. I'm calmer now, more relaxed, less anxious. And I find that it feels good to just listen to the silence. What a great reminder that just because you don't hear something, it doesn't mean that something isn't happening.

Elijah's Story

There is a famous story in the Old Testament about God speaking through silence to Elijah, one of His prophets. You can read the whole story in I Kings 18–19, but here's a summary: Elijah has a dramatic victory over the prophets of the false god Baal. It is such a great and amazing victory that the people who had been worshipping Baal now bow to the ground and shout, "In your face, Baal! God is the One True God!"

However, when the wicked Queen Jezebel hears about this, she points her long, green, bony finger in the air and says, "I'll get you my pretty, and your little dog, too!" (That's how I always picture Jezebel in the Bible.) When Elijah hears about her threat, he becomes completely dominated by fear, even though he just had that awesome victory from God. Fear takes his focus off God and puts it on his circumstances. His perspective is that this great victory didn't change a thing. The God-hating queen still has power over the people, the idols are still safely on their thrones, and the people are still blindly honoring Baal and dishonoring God. He doesn't see God at work, and his faith falters.

Elijah feels completely alone in this battle, so he decides to retreat. He doesn't just run away to save his life; he runs to get away from a ministry that, to him, looks like a complete failure. He runs away from unfulfilled expectations. He runs to a place where he can hide from all his disappointment and discouragement.

Elijah runs until he collapses from exhaustion. Before he falls asleep, he has just enough energy to pray, "You might as well just take me home now because I'm not doing any good here."

You've been there, right? You've found yourself in a dark time. After 25 years of a marriage that you thought was good, your husband confesses to an affair. You invest time and creativity in your company, but your boss doesn't value your input and chooses someone less qualified for the promotion. Your oncologist discovers a new suspicious spot, and you prepare for round three of chemo. In your dark time, whatever it may be, you fall across your bed and say, "I don't even know what else I can do. I give up. I'm tired of thinking about this, and I can't take it anymore. If this is the way life is going to be, then I'm done."

Do you think these words surprise God? Do you think you and Elijah are the only ones who have threatened to throw in the towel? Look at what Moses says to God when the Israelites keep complaining:

> "I can't do this by myself—it's too much, all these people. If this is how you intend to treat me, do me a favor and kill me. I've seen enough. I've had enough. Let me out of here." (Numbers 11:15 MSG).

And look at what the prophet Jeremiah says:

"He should have killed me before I was born ... Why, oh why, did I ever leave that womb? Life's been nothing but trouble and tears." (Jeremiah 20:17–18 MSG).

And the prophet Jonah, when the prophecy God told him to preach does not happen:

"Just kill me now, Lord! I'd rather be dead than alive if what I predicted will not happen."" (Jonah 4:3).

God's Story

Everyone has times of deep discouragement. Times where the pain wears us down, and we just want to say, "Enough already!" God understands when we are physically and emotionally depleted. Notice what He does in Elijah's weary despair: He lets him sleep. Sometimes the most important thing you can do when your burdens are heavy beyond your endurance is to come to a complete rest.

"It is useless for you to work so hard from early morning until late at night, anxiously working for food to eat; for God gives rest to his loved ones." (Psalm 127:2).

Check out what God doesn't do when Elijah says "I'm done. Just done." He doesn't chide or scold Elijah. He doesn't call him a baby and tell him to snap out of it. He doesn't give him the silent treatment or shame him for being depressed. And most of all, He doesn't leave him alone. He allows Elijah to sleep and rest. God stays right beside him, and when it is time to eat, He wakes Elijah up with a gentle touch and says, "How about some freshly baked bread and some cool refreshing water?" After he eats and drinks, God says, "One more nap," and allows him to go back to sleep to prepare for the journey ahead.

Our God is a compassionate God. Even if you don't see Him or hear Him, God is always right beside you. He understands your physical weakness and your emotional sadness.

He doesn't scold you for your lack of faith or your accusations that He doesn't understand how you feel. You can be assured in your dark moments that He will tenderly and carefully begin the work of restoring your soul and body when you don't even know what to pray, when you are tired and ready to give up, and when you wonder why He is so silent.

When God wakes Elijah up a second time, He encourages him to eat some more and then allows him to go to Mount Sinai—the mountain of God. God wants him to get to a place where he can learn a very important truth—the truth that just because God doesn't work the way you expect, it doesn't mean that He isn't at work at all. His purpose is breathtakingly deeper than you could ever dream! And His glory is awe-inspiring higher than you could ever imagine!

"My thoughts are nothing like your thoughts," says the Lord. "And my ways are far beyond anything you could imagine. For just as the heavens are higher than the earth, so my ways are higher than your ways and my thoughts higher than your thoughts." (Isaiah 55:8–9).

Elijah runs to the **mountain of God** and **spends the night** in a cave. Check out the two phrases that I highlighted. Elijah chose to **spend his dark time** at the **mountain of God**. Even though Elijah feels like God left him, he decides to run to Him. Elijah's mood hadn't changed; he is still very disappointed and disillusioned. But perhaps he knows that the best place to be when his life is in turmoil is the mountain of God. And it is in that dark cave that God spoke to him.

My Story

I don't remember everything that happened once my cancer treatment started, but perhaps my worst memory lapse was on the day after my back surgery when they biopsied the tumor. Phil and Phillip (our 27-year-old son) stayed with me all morning, and I remember being happy they were there. We talked about all the nice phone calls of support they had received, and all the great comments and prayers people had posted on Facebook for our family and for me. I was in and out of sleep, so after one of my drug-induced conversations about seeing wigs all around the room, they decided to let me rest while they went to lunch.

At lunch, Phillip told his dad that it scared him a little to hear my crazy talk. Phil assured him that it was just the medicine talking and not to worry. He told Phillip just to stay calm and that pretty soon I would fall back to sleep and most likely forget everything I said or "saw."

Later that night, I felt alert enough to see what was going on in the Facebook world. I wanted to read what the guys had been talking about that morning. The first post I saw was Phillip's, and it said, "We received the final diagnosis—Mom has CNS Lymphoma Stage 4." I thought, "Why would Phillip post that? It sounds like he is saying I have cancer. Oh, no. Now everyone is going to think I have cancer!" I looked up Phil's post, and it said the same thing.

Suddenly a whirlwind of emotions and thoughts began swirling around in my mind. I thought, "Are they saying I have cancer? That's not right. I must not be reading this correctly." I kept trying to concentrate on what I was reading, but the words were deafening, and everything felt so loud and confusing. I couldn't make sense of it. I called Phil, but it was late, and he didn't answer. I thought he had gone to sleep. I looked at the words again and tried to figure it out on my own, but I couldn't remember anything about being told I had cancer. I felt desperate to know what was going on! Then I realized I could call Phillip. He usually stays up late. He answered, and I dreaded what I was going to have to ask him.

I tried to hold it together as I said, "Phillip, I have to ask you a tough question." He said "OK," and just waited. I said, "Do I have cancer? Because …" (the dam broke, and I started crying heavily) "… no one told me I had cancer." I suddenly realized that I knew in my heart what he was going to say. Just like his dad had prepared him earlier in the day and from an inner strength that God clearly gave him, he calmly and softly said, "Yes, Mom, you do." I kept crying and asked him, "Why didn't I know, and why didn't anyone tell me?" He said, "Well, Mom, you did know, but you don't remember because of all the medicine you are on." I don't think I had ever heard my son talk so gently and comfortingly to me. I cried and cried. Phillip told me about my cancer and what my treatment would be. I kept trying to remember, and he continued to remind me that I would remember when the drugs were out of my system. His tenderness comforted me, and he prayed for me before we hung up.

Back to Elijah's Story

Elijah spends the night in his dark cave. But God is with him (as He always had been), and He speaks to him: "Come here, Elijah. I want to tell you something." As soon as Elijah comes to the mouth of the cave, a tremendous hurricane sweeps through with such force that it tears out chunks of the mountain, and boulders come tumbling down around him. As Elijah takes shelter at the edge of the cave, an earthquake began rolling under his feet and starts shaking the earth. Nothing feels stable. As soon as the shaking of the earthquake stops, there is fire. Lightning illuminates the entire sky, and as each bolt kisses the earth, vegetation is ignited, and flames sweep from ridge to ridge. Soon the heavens and earth are ablaze with God's glory. Elijah's spirit is fully awakened now, and he stands confidently while the wind blows, the earth shakes, and fire flashes all around him. He knows he is in the presence of God Almighty, and he eagerly waits to hear God speak.

But God's voice is not in the fire, or the earthquake, or the whirlwind. It is when the fire dies out, and the earth stops shaking, and the wind stops roaring that God chooses to speak. There is nothing more powerful than the quiet after a loud uproar. Out of that quiet, still air comes what the Hebrews call "a voice of gentle silence," as if silence has become audible.

God chooses to speak to Elijah in that still small voice to remind him that even though he is going through a dark time, and even though the situation hasn't worked out the way he expected or wanted, God has not abandoned him. Even though Elijah feels alone, he isn't. God has been there all along. And God still has a purpose and plan for him.

Back to My Story

In the flurry of all my tests, procedures, and doctors, I wanted God to shout His will for me in everything I read and heard about my cancer. I wanted to know what would happen to me and when and how things would happen. I wanted to know my prognosis. I wondered if I would ever walk again. I cried thinking that I might never get to know my new granddaughter and that she would only know about me from pictures and stories. I struggled with the burden that I would be to Phil.

But in those first few days, God said to me, "Come here, Melody. I want to tell you something." Like a whisper in my ear, God told me, "This is not about you. This is going to be about how I can be glorified in this part of your life's journey. You don't need to know the details because I've already got it covered. You can trust Me." It's not the plan I would have chosen, but God reminded me daily that He had a purpose for my life that was greater than cancer.

"This is God's Word on the subject … "I'll show up and take care of you as I promised and bring you back home. I know what I'm doing. I have it all planned out—plans to take care of you, not abandon you, plans to give you the future you hope for. When you call on me, when you come and pray to me, I'll listen. When you come looking for me, you'll find me. Yes, when you get serious about finding me and want it more than anything else, I'll make sure you won't be disappointed." (Jeremiah 29:10–14 MSG).

Are you allowing fear, stress, or adversity to drown out God's whisper in your ear? Is your focus on the whirlwind and your glance on the working of God? Of course, God *could* speak to us with the volume turned way up, and sometimes that is how He speaks. But if He always shouted, listening wouldn't be required. When God chooses to whisper, I think it's because He wants us to pay attention. He wants us to be very close to Him. A whispered message requires us to be near to the Whisperer and to be quiet and still enough to recognize His voice. There is an intimacy in a whispered message. More than anything else, God wants an intimate relationship with you. You will not experience an intimate relationship with someone you haven't spent time with. And what better way to walk through a dark time than with the Friend who sticks closer than a brother?

I had two therapists whom I especially liked in the rehab hospital. After my first full day, just as I was thinking that I hoped I would get those two as my therapists every day, they both ran over to me and said they had requested to be assigned to my case. That made me feel so good! One was my physical therapist who was helping me get my strength back, and the other was my occupational therapist who was helping me learn the skills I would need to take care of myself at home. I was still a little shy and nervous when I went into rehab, but since God had already told me that this wasn't about me, I decided

I needed to get to know these two sweet girls better. I asked my OT about her family, how long she had been an OT, and where she lived. It turned out that she lived in the same city that we did. Before I could ask her, she asked me where we went to church. Since there are literally hundreds of churches in our city, I thought it would be a long shot for her to even recognized the name. As soon as I said my church's name, her eyes lit up, and she said that was her church home! She even knew my granddaughter, Emma, since she volunteered with the babies, and she knew my son and daughter-in-law, too. What an unexpected blessing! During my three weeks in rehab, we prayed for each other, and I loved being able to encourage her in her walk with Christ.

My PT was a little quieter and more reserved. She was not going to church at the time, but she was getting married in two weeks. I congratulated and celebrated with her, which led me to ask about her family. She told me that her father had passed away from a fast-moving cancer—the same kind I had—just six weeks earlier. Now I knew why she had a sadness about her, even though she was doing her best to stay upbeat and encouraging about my progress. We talked a lot. She asked me about my diagnosis and prognosis, and I asked her about her dad's cancer. He had an allergic reaction to the chemo and became very sick. Even though they stopped the chemo, he never regained his strength and passed away quickly.

We talked about her mom, her brother, and how the family was coping. We talked about what her wedding would be like without her dad there. She had been very close to her dad. Then she asked me, "Aren't you scared?" I could tell it took a lot of courage for her to ask, and I knew exactly what she was referring to. I thought for a moment and said, "Well, I don't really feel like throwing a party, but I know that my days were all numbered before I was born, and if this is my time to go, I'm ready. Stomping my foot and being angry about the situation isn't going to change anything. Besides,

I know for sure that I'm going to heaven, and I don't want to stand before God knowing that I wasted my last days on earth feeling sorry for myself."

I knew she was taking it all in. We talked about eternity a lot. I talked about how I feel the presence of my mom and dad, who had already passed, around me all the time. And I wanted her to know that even though her dad wouldn't get to dance with her at her wedding, he would be there in spirit—cheering her on, telling her that she was a wonderful daughter, that he was proud of her. I got to pray with her a couple of times, and other times I told her I was praying. As it turned out, she was doing her internship in that rehab facility and was only there for six weeks. I was with her for two of those weeks. God orchestrated that precisely.

If I didn't have an intimate relationship with God, I could have easily wasted the time God gave me with these two girls. But because I have been putting my spiritual roots deep down into the Word of God since I was 16 years old, I have learned to recognize God's voice in the dark times of my life. And just as He whispered to me that He loved me and had a plan and purpose for my life even with cancer, He nudged me in the direction of these two sweet women and told me exactly how to pray for them.

Start Your Own Story

Wouldn't you like to know God so intimately that you could hear Him in the noisy and silent places of your life? It doesn't take much. You can use the formula I have used and shared with others for years.

1. Pick a Time
2. Pick a Place
3. Pick a Plan

Pick a Time

Choose a time of the day to devote to reading your Bible and spending a few minutes in prayer. This doesn't require setting aside hours. Start with just a few minutes. Maybe the best part of your day to have for just you and God is in the morning, a few minutes before the rest of the family gets up. Maybe it's in the middle of your day when your kids are napping or lunch time if you are at work. It could be the last thing you do before bed, when the house is finally quiet. The time of day doesn't matter as much as keeping it the same time every day. Soon that time becomes sacred, or set apart, for you and God.

Pick a Place

Find a place in your home where you can be comfortable and relaxed. It could be in your favorite chair in the living room, or at the dining room table, or on your bed. When you pick that place, determine to have your alone time with God there every day. Then, every time you pass that place, you'll remember that God wants to meet you there. You have a standing appointment with Him that you don't want to miss.

Pick a Plan

There are so many wonderful places in the Scripture to read. However, putting your Bible on your lap, allowing it to fall open, and plunging your finger blindly down on the page to see where you will read that day (my friend calls this "the Holy dip") isn't the best reading plan. Just search "Bible Reading Plans" online, and you will find a multitude of options. Download the YouVersion Bible app to your phone, and you will find a nearly unlimited supply of devotions. Pick a plan and stick with it. You will be amazed at how God speaks to you each day when you sit down and decide—even in a dark time—to discover God's presence and learn to recognize His voice.

Tools For Your Time With God

Bible - or the YouVersion Bible app on your phone

Journal and Pen - First, before you begin reading, sit quietly and write down questions you have for God. Second, read your devotional and Scriptures. Lastly, Journal anything you believe God is telling you to do. Expect God to say something, and when He does, write it down. Don't miss this step. We all tend to think we will remember everything God says, but I promise you won't. So, write it down!

Separate pad of paper - As soon as you sit down for your undisturbed time with God, you'll start thinking of things to do: put clothes in the dryer, email your mother about a party, set out the meat to thaw for dinner, etc. If you get up and do those "quick" things, your time with God will never happen. The enemy would rather have you distracted than determined! So, write down the things you don't want to forget on the separate pad of paper and get right back to your devotion.

Tissues - You'll need them on the days you get emotional over the Scripture or life circumstances that you are bringing to God. They are also nice to have on hand because when I look down for a long period of time, my nose runs! Believe me—the enemy doesn't want you to be encouraged or to embrace the promises of God. It's just another distraction to have to get up and find a tissue, so have them there when you first sit down.

It's as simple as that. Did you know that there are over *6,000* promises from God to you in the Bible? I embraced many of them as I journeyed through the dark moment of cancer. God wants you to know and claim His promises for yourself. He says that when you seek Him, you WILL find Him. He doesn't try to trick you or make it hard. You don't have to wait until you are in church. He is not interested in memorized quotes or prayers. He wants you to just talk to Him.

Are you confused about the direction to take in your career? **Ask Him.** Have you been betrayed by a good friend? **Tell Him.** Are you frustrated about disciplining your strong-willed child, or are you burdened for your adult child? **Talk to Him.** Are you struggling with a secret sin and see no way out? **Call on Him.** Has your beloved been given a diagnosis of a terminal illness with a prognosis of 3 more months? **Cry out to Him.** Are you lonely? Do you feel like God is far away from you? Are you afraid that God has turned His back on you? **Pray to Him.**

He sees you, and He hears you. His greatest desire is that you become so intimately acquainted with Him that you hear His whisper, His "voice of gentle silence" in your dark time.

Let me demonstrate what happens when you decide to start listening to God's voice. The morning that I was putting some finishing touches on this chapter, I didn't know how I was going to bring it to a close. I was impressed to end with a Scripture of promise for you. I use the YouVersion Bible app that I mentioned earlier. When you open the app, the first thing you see is the verse of the day. I opened the app, but I skipped that page and clicked right to the reading section to start looking through some verses I had highlighted. But then I felt a gentle nudge to click back to the verse of the day. Look at what God had planned from the beginning of time as today's verse of the day:

> *"This is what the Lord says—the Lord who made the earth, who formed and established it, whose name is the Lord: 'Ask me and I will tell you remarkable **secrets** you do not know about things to come.'" (Jeremiah 33:2–3).*

When I think of the word "secret," I think of something being whispered. God is so personal with me that on the day I was writing about hearing God's still, small voice, He chose to direct me to a verse that makes a promise about how He speaks to us. When we ask Him, when we lift our voice to Him, He not only hears us, but He whispers secrets in our ears. Raise your hand if that gives you goose bumps and chills! I can't see you, but that's ok. God can!

Wouldn't you like to have that kind of relationship with the God of creation? Start today! It's never too late to start tuning your ear to Him. You're never too old; you're never too far gone; you're never too messed up. He simply says, "Ask Me." And when you do, He cares so deeply for you that He promises to answer. That can be your first promise to claim and write in your journal.

Section Three

GOD CARES FOR YOU

CHAPTER 7

"*My Precious.*"

The Lord of the Rings

I f there is only one thing I know for sure, it is that we will not get through this life without going through dark times. Some of those dark times come upon us without warning. A loved one dies instantly from a brain aneurysm; a wife discovers an email that reveals an illicit affair; a simple call into the boss's office becomes the last day at work. Suddenly, your world is spinning, you can't find your bearings, and you are moving in slow motion.

In the early days, before we had a diagnosis for the pain in my legs, I experienced the frustration of not knowing if we would ever find an answer. Darkness loomed over me every morning. And even though I knew the doctors were looking for proof of cancer so they would know how to proceed, the actual words, "Yes. It's what we thought. You have cancer," hit me like a thunder clap of the loudest decibels.

Several years ago, Phil and I were sitting and talking in our living room on a scorching hot Texas afternoon. I was in a chair next to the front picture window, and Phil was on the sofa across from me. Out of the blue (literally, the sky was blue), it suddenly felt like the air was sucked out of the room. We felt our house rumble, and the sheer curtains covering the picture window puffed out into the room as if King Kong had taken a step on the street outside our house, causing the curtains to react to the force of his foot. It took only a split second after seeing the curtains rise and fall for me to comprehend that something very bad was about to happen. I couldn't move fast enough to get away from the picture window! In what felt like slow motion, I lifted myself out of the chair as I heard the biggest, loudest, deepest, strongest (ALL the "ests") thunder clap I had ever heard in my life! My insides rumbled like I was sitting too close to the speakers at a rock concert, and I thought that at any moment I would hear and feel glass shattering all over my back as I fell into Phil's arms.

I'll come back to this story a little later, but I think it's a pretty good illustration of how it feels when we are instantly and without warning plunged into a dark moment.

Some dark moments reveal themselves slowly over time: a lingering depression as one more month passes of not being able to get pregnant; a longing for an unfulfilled goal that seems harder to achieve day after day; an inability to get control over an addiction that threatens to destroy your reputation or your family; caring for a loved one with a slow, debilitating terminal illness, knowing that no matter what you do, this one you love so much will not get better.

Phil and I were unsure about so many things in the days before the cancer diagnosis. One very late night, I started writing an update on Facebook. I was mostly just recording my thoughts as I tried to figure out how to navigate the darkness. That single post received more comments than anything I had ever written. Since it had such an impact on so many, I thought I'd include it in this book:

New symptoms have developed in my foot. From the research I've done, it might mean another MRI. It most definitely will need some specialized physical therapy. There is more pain and significantly greater numbness. And while I know this isn't the worst thing in the whole world, I have to be honest: I kind of want to cry about it. (Just as I typed that last sentence, a big tear formed in my right eye. Which is funny because I'm on several medicines that calm the nerves in my legs but also calm my emotions, so I CAN'T cry! Hmmm, thinking about that ... I hope I will be able to cry at the wedding. Mary will be sad if I don't. Oh well, her dad and her husband-to-be Matthew will cry enough for all of us!

I just thought of an old country song: "There are tears in my ears from lying on my back in my bed when I cry over you."[14] I've done that. Haven't you?

Speaking from a woman's point of view, it feels good to cry loudly when you're by yourself until you just have a few heavy breaths of a whimper. The kind of cry that says, "I'm so tired of this! This hurts too much! I don't understand why I'm not getting better! I'm tired of not being able to just bend over and pick up something on the floor; of not being able to stand up from the sofa without assistance; of not being able to drive a car yet; of not being able to carry the laundry to the laundry room; of not being able to get in or out of a pool; of not being able to drive over and see my grandbaby!!!!!" That's what that loud, long cry is saying!

For me, once it's over—the crying, not the situation—I'm good. I'm a Christ follower. And I believe the Bible. In Psalms, David writes that God collects all our tears and saves them in a bottle. Why? Because they are precious to Him. He hears our crying and is so close to us during that time that He collects them in a jar. I imagine that He writes our name on the jar and also writes the date and situation we were crying over. Then when we get to heaven and He talks to us and answers questions for us, He shows us all the jars. We will be amazed at how detailed He is! And how loving and caring, seeing how the things that brought pain to us on earth brought pain to Him, too. I'm not sure when it happens, but maybe then our eyes are opened to why we had a certain sickness, why we lost a baby, why our depressed son took his own life, why a spouse was killed by a drunk driver.

Maybe then we will have God's perspective that "all things work together for good to those are called according to His purpose."[15] And then we begin to put back those jars of tears with thankfulness and praise in our heart and adoration on our face as we kneel in worship in a way we never have before! That will be a beautiful day!

A couple of weeks ago, I found 3 small jars in a junk drawer. Each jar had someone's name on it—Paul, Mary, and Phillip. I wondered what I had saved. I opened them and found baby teeth! Why did I save them? Because it reminded me of a sweet time when I got physically close to them, comforted them, and celebrated with them as they received money from the tooth fairy! Good things come from difficult things.

That's a nice memory. I asked Mary if she wanted her jar of teeth. She politely and demurely declined, saying, "No, gross, Mom!" Ok. I can only assume the memory of her teeth falling out is still all too painful.

Now what was I saying? Am I still in the parenthesis? Oh! I am! Longest parenthesis in the history of FB. Wonder if I get a prize for that!?)

Ok, why did I start this post? I don't know. My scattered thoughts in the parenthesis seem to have helped me. I like thinking about those teeth in the jars and how they remind me about God collecting our tears. (And I like thinking how it's going to gross the kids out when I wrap them up for Christmas and give it to them!!!)

You Are Precious to God

Sometimes the hardest question to answer, whether you are suddenly plunged into a dark time or whether the darkness is slow and lingering, is if God truly cares for you. You know He sees you, and you believe He hears you—but does He really care about what is going on in your life? At the time that I wrote the above Facebook post, just knowing that God is collecting my tears in a jar answered the question of His care in my life. It is such a tender picture of a loving Father feeling the pain I felt. But I'll be honest and admit that since that time, I've had other low moments, and I have asked, "Lord, don't You care?" Just three days after I wrote chapter 6 of this book, I had a conversation with Phil about some difficult things going on in our lives not nearly as dark as our days walking through my cancer treatment. In my panic, I was basically asking God, "Don't You see that this is unfair? Don't You care about what is happening?" A couple of days later, I sat down to start writing again, and I re-read Chapter 6 to see where I left off. I was immediately convicted of my anxious questioning of God's ways, and I said to Phil, "Who wrote this chapter? Because it certainly wasn't me!"

No matter what circumstances you are faced with—stress at work, not enough money in the bank to pay the bills, a crumbling marriage, a dysfunctional relationship, an unsettling diagnosis—God cares. And no matter how many times you ask God, "Do You see what is happening to me? Do You hear my prayers, my constant plea to You? Do You even care?" the answer is always, "Yes. I care, My child. I care more than you can even know."

God answers this question of how much He cares over and over in the Bible, but my favorite book of the Bible (my "go-to" book, especially in times of disappointment or discouragement) is Psalms. This book was mostly written by King David, a prolific songwriter and journal-er. (Ha! I use the word "prolific" like I'm such a good wordsmith and then "journal-er" to prove not so much.) David's songs are raw, real, and reflective, and I honestly relate to so many.

Put your finger on almost any chapter in Psalms, and you will find comfort and inspiration to trust God no matter what circumstances you are going through. You'll identify with his questions as he pleads with God and says that he is *"worn out from sobbing,"* and his bed is *"drenched with tears"(Psalm 6:6).* I've done that a few times. Have you? David says that his *"vision is blurred by grief" (Psalm 6:7).* I've felt blinded by grief. Haven't you? David asks, *"O Lord, why do you stand so far away? Why do you hide when I am in trouble?" (Psalm 10:1).* He asks, *"O Lord, how long will you forget me? Forever? How long will you look the other way?" (Psalm 13:1).* I've wondered where God is at times. What about you?

David's songs are also songs of love, thankfulness, and praise. He writes in *Psalm 27:1 that the Lord is his light in a dark time, so why should he be afraid?* (I agree!) He encourages us to sing praises to the Lord because His favor lasts a lifetime. He says, *"Weeping may last through the night, but joy comes with the morning" (Psalm 30:5).* He instructs the listener to pay attention to the many wonders that the Lord has done. When you do, you will be amazed, and you will put your trust in Him. (I've experienced that!) Oh, as I am scrolling right now through Psalms on my smart phone, I don't want to stop! It's all so good. From the most loved and familiar Psalm (Psalm 23) to the most unknown and obscure, you can hear David's voice as he pleads with God, and you will find yourself saying, "Me, too!"

David loved music and had many on his worship team. Asaph was one of his worship leaders, and 12 of the Psalms are attributed to him. Psalm 77 is a beautiful song that reveals God's understanding of our questions, our fears, and our despair in dark moments.

You Can Be Honest With God

Psalm 77 begins the way many of the songs in the book of Psalms do: with raw emotion and honesty. We don't know the situation behind Asaph's anguish, but does it matter? To me, it doesn't. What ministers to me is the way he expresses himself during an obviously dark time. He cries, he shouts, he begs God to listen to him. All night long he prays with his hands outstretched to God. He moans and is overwhelmed with longing for God to help. He can't sleep; he can't even put his thoughts into words.

And then he asks questions, questions that expose his fear of being abandoned by God:

Is God finished with me and put me on a shelf?
Will I ever experience God's blessings on my life again?
Where is His unfailing love that I've experienced before?
Are His promises even true?
Has God forgotten me?
Is He mad at me?
Does He even care about me?

Sometimes when our pain is at its most intense and we are done, just done, we ask questions. We might even add our own questions to this list. Is God really there? If He is there, why is He allowing this to happen? Do I really deserve this?

Asaph isn't ashamed to be asking these questions. When we have these questions on our hearts, God knows it, so we might as well voice them. It's when we are honest with God about our feelings, our worries, our fear, our anger, our doubt, and our disappointment that God can speak to us. You won't hurt God's feelings by being honest with Him about how you feel. So, let it out!

After this time of questioning, in the space of two sentences, he turns everything around. While tossing and turning in his bed, unable to sleep, he makes a declaration. He says,

91

"This is my issue, not God's. I am struggling with the thoughts that God has turned against me." (dramatic pause) *"But then I recall all you have done, O Lord"* (Psalm 77:11). In the midst of pain and darkness, stuck between what he believes and how he feels, Asaph determines to remember the good things God has done in the past and the truth of who God is right now. He forces himself to recall the past blessings of God on his life, rehearse in worship who God is in the present, and rejoice as hope for the future is strengthened.

A few years ago, Paul and Meredith (our son and daughter-in-law) decided to sell their house and downsize to a smaller home. They did this for several reasons, one of which was to have the freedom to give more to their church's building fund. They quickly found a house that was smaller, older, and a bit of a fixer upper. Just before they moved in, I asked Meredith how she was doing with the move. She told me that even though she was very much committed to this decision, she found herself listing out loud to Paul all the things she didn't like about the new house right after they purchased it. She said, "This went on for a couple of days, and finally Paul just looked at me and said he was tired of hearing the complaints and that I could only name three more things that I didn't like. After that, he told me I could only talk about the good things about our move and our house." I said, "Wow! What did you say?" She said, "I thought to myself, 'Oh, no! Only three more things? I better make them really good!'" That makes me laugh.

Despite how Meredith felt about the house, she believed that this new house was the answer to a specific prayer. She went on to tell me that she did start listing all the good things, and that turned her outlook around. Between how she felt and what she believed, she made a choice to trust God.

You Can Determine to Trust God

Read the shift in Asaph's song:

"And I said, "This is my fate; the Most High has turned his hand against me." **But then I recall all you have done, O Lord**; *I remember your wonderful deeds of long ago. They are constantly in my thoughts. I cannot stop thinking about your mighty works."* (Psalm 77:10–12).

In the first few verses of Psalm 77, Asaph is lamenting to someone … anyone! His focus is completely on his problem and how God seems to have forgotten him and is nowhere to be found. And while God welcomes his honesty, his complaining does nothing for his circumstances or his attitude, except make him feel even worse. Then suddenly, in the midst of his darkness and feeling like God had abandoned him, Asaph shifts his focus from himself to God. He changes his linear outlook to a vertical one, and for the rest of this song, he is singing directly to God. Asaph decides to remember and meditate on all the things God has done. And as he does this, his frame of mind is dramatically changed.

This is why it is so important for you to journal! A journal is not a diary, not "This is what I ate today. This is who I talked to today. This is where I went today." A journal is a place to record the things God is teaching you. It's where you ask questions and use Scriptures to answer those questions. When you are going through a difficult time, you can always go back and read how God was real and personal to you and how He spoke to you in a previous dark time. I know you think that if God speaks to you, you will never forget it, so it is not necessary to write it down. But you do forget, and you will forget. Just take my word for it. Write it down.

When you are up against emotional pressures and discouragement, especially on those difficult days when everything seems to go wrong and your faith is tried to the limit, you will be able to go back to your journal and think about the activity of God in your life. In those recorded stories of your life and from the stories in the Scripture, you will always find something that jumps off the page and helps you more than anything else. Asaph's one thing is the story of the Israelites crossing the Red Sea. In that story, Asaph can claim for himself that God is always sovereign over all human events.

As Asaph recalls what it must have been like for the Israelites to walk the pathway through the Red Sea, he imagines their fear. Between two great walls of water, lightning flashed, thunder crashed, and the earth rumbled and rolled. He writes that while the Israelites were afraid of the sights and sounds around them, they also walked in faith, knowing that these forces were all God's and under His control. *("Your arrows of lightning flashed. Your thunder roared from the whirlwind" [Psalm 77:17–18].)* The events that frighten you today are all under the control and authority of God. There will be days of pressure and times of trial when everything seems to be going wrong, and nothing is going as expected. The knowledge that every force, natural or human, is under the control of God will keep you and give you the assurance needed to get through the darkness. You can trust Him because He is in control.

Asaph looks again at the story of the Red Sea crossing. The Israelites could see God's hand as He prepared the way, sending plagues upon Egypt that eventually softened the heart of Pharaoh to let them leave. They recognized God's leadership through Moses and Aaron and did everything they told them, which allowed them to plunder the Egyptians on their way out. They saw God leading with a pillar of cloud by day and a pillar of fire by night. But when they looked up and saw all of Pharaoh's army chasing after them, they panicked.

They saw that they were stuck between the Red Sea and all of Pharaoh's troops, and they didn't understand what God was doing. When they could identify God's ways, it was easy to trust Him. But when His way was undefinable, unknowable, they got scared. They complained, blamed Moses and Aaron, and cried about wishing they had never left Egypt. Asaph remembers that part of the story, but he also knows the end of it. God had planned all along to guide them through the Red Sea to safety. This was His intention when they left Egypt, and He had it in mind all the way. The Israelites could not see that. It never entered their minds. But God knew it. As Asaph thinks about this, he uncovers another great truth: the inability to understand how God is working does not mean that He is not at work.

"Your road led through the sea, your pathway through the mighty waters—a pathway no one knew was there!" (Psalm 77:19).

Asaph writes these words because they are a special comfort to him. At the beginning of this song, Asaph is in distress and deep trouble, and it seems to him like God is doing nothing. He believes that God sees and hears him, but does He really care? As Asaph reflects on the events of the crossing of the Red Sea, he sees a parallel experience to what he is going through. As the Israelites reached the edge of the Red Sea, there was no visible way out, no human alternative they could see. But God knew the answer all the time. Though His footprints were unseen and they could not predict what He was going to do, the outcome proved that God knew what He was doing. Even when you can't see God's hand, you can trust His ways and His path and know that He cares.

Imagine with me as Asaph leads the orchestra and choir to sing this song of the wonders of God and the demonstration of His awesome power. With each lyric of praise that sings of God's rescue of the Israelites through the Red Sea, the music becomes louder and more driving. When the musicians sing of the arrows of lightning and the thunder from the whirlwind, the percussion section takes center stage. The music continues to swell to the highest crescendo; then, suddenly, a breathtaking musical rest where no notes are played, and the conductor's staff is frozen mid-air. The congregation and the musicians are silent and expectant, waiting and watching for Asaph's gentle downbeat, leading them to sing softly and play earnestly the last line of God's care for His people like a shepherd caring for his sheep. Read the following and see if you can imagine it with me.

> *"Oh God, your ways are holy. Is there any god as mighty as you? You are the God of great wonders! You demonstrate your awesome power among the nations. By your strong arm, you redeemed your people, the descendants of Jacob and Joseph. Interlude[.]When the Red Sea saw You, O God, its waters looked and trembled! The sea quaked to its very depths. The clouds poured down rain; the thunder rumbled in the sky. Your arrows of lightning flashed. Your thunder roared from the whirlwind; the lightning lit up the world! The earth trembled and shook. Your road led through the sea, your pathway through the mighty waters—a pathway no one knew was there!*
>
> *[musical rest]*
>
> *You led your people along that road like a flock of sheep, with Moses and Aaron as their shepherds."* (Psalm 77:13–20).

You Can Be Certain of God's Care for You

You may be asking, "Does God care?" You may be thinking, "He has so many other things to care about in this world. Does He really care about me?" I want you to remember that God cares for you the way a shepherd cares for his sheep. A shepherd cares tenderly, leading his sheep to green pastures and fresh waters to eat and drink. When they are hurt, he carries them on his back and cradles them in his arms. When one strays, the shepherd seeks for it until it is found. He watches over the sheep day and night to protect them from predators. The shepherd counts his sheep each night because each one is precious to him.

God cares because He created you.

"I am your Creator. You were in my care even before you were born" (Isaiah 44:2 CEV).

God cares for you so much that He planned every day of your life in advance, choosing the exact time you would be born and the exact time of your death.

"You saw me before I was born. Every day of my life was recorded in your book. Every moment was laid out before a single day had passed." (Psalm 139:16).

Before the world was even made, God loved you and cared for you.

"Long before He laid down earth's foundations, he had us in mind, had settled on us as the focus of his love." (Ephesians 1:4 MSG).

And God will continue to care for you until your dying day.

"I have carried you since you were born; I have taken care of you from your birth. Even when you are old, I will be the same. Even when your hair has turned gray, I will take care of you. I made you and will take care of you." (Isaiah 46:3–4 NCV).

Meanwhile, back to that hot summer day and the loud thunder …

Did the picture window explode with a shower of glass all over us? Had a tree been struck, and had it fallen and crashed into our house?

Oh, how I wish this had a better ending. After I fell into Phil's arms, we both waited breathlessly. I opened my eyes that had been squeezed tightly shut and slowly turned around. I was not covered in glass; the picture window was still intact, and everything was completely normal in our living room. We went to look outside. I was sure I would see that a tree had fallen over, or a sink hole had opened up and a neighbor's house was gone, or at least a meteor the size of the Dallas Cowboys' stadium had plummeted into our neighborhood. I just knew all of our neighbors would be out on the street trying to figure out what happened. Nope. Nothing had changed. And we were the only ones in our yard with quizzical looks on our face. It was as if nothing had happened. At all! To be honest, if I was going to be that scared, I wanted to see some damage, some evidence that something had actually happened.

As I look back on this experience (and I can still feel the fear I felt then as if it just happened!), I realize that the reason I jumped into Phil's arms was that it is in those arms that I found safety, protection, and comfort. And I saw in his eyes that he cared for me.

When the dark clouds of uncertainty form in your life and it seems like the end of the world, there is One who cares for you and is waiting for you to turn to Him and jump into His arms. You can be sure that underneath the apparent inactivity of God is a shepherd's love, protection, and care. He sees you, He hears you, and He cares for you more than you can possibly imagine.

CHAPTER 8

"Fasten your seatbelts, it's going to be a bumpy night."

All About Eve

My husband, Phil, was my primary caregiver through the three years of my illness. I asked him to write this chapter as an encouragement to other caregivers and their loved ones.

B eing a caregiver doesn't always happen overnight. And whenever the role comes, it always seems to ask more of us than we ever imagined. It's a tough job. Some have it for a while, others for a lifetime. Regardless of the length of serving, most caretakers seem to agree that we each go through the same physical and emotional struggles and questions of faith.

My caretaking only lasted about three years, including the recovery time. Melody's illness started almost two years before her cancer diagnosis. She started having nerve issues in her neck, arm, and back. After months of tests up and down her back, doctors told us it was not a back issue. The arm and back troubles subsided. She developed Trigeminal Neuralgia (TN), which brings horrible pain in the ear and down the jaw. TN is often called the "suicide disease" as many people cannot handle the extreme pain. Determined to push through it, Melody performed a hilarious routine in front of 7,000 people. We were so grateful when God answered our prayers and healed her from it, saving her from a lifetime of agony.

After her battle with TN, Melody noticed there might be another issue. One day, she stepped up on a curb, and her leg seemed weak. This initial weakness developed into debilitating pain, first in one leg and then in the other. The next 13 months consisted of a series of infusions, two stays in the hospital (totaling 28 days), nerve biopsies on her leg, and countless days in bed. Eventually, all the medications stopped working, and we finally had the diagnosis of Stage 4, Central Nervous System (CNS) Lymphoma. Only three percent of all lymphoma patients develop this form. Even rarer was the fact that it was only in her spinal cord.

Melody spent 23 days in rehab, learning how to take care of herself while I was at work. She then had eight chemo treatments over the next six months. She had to stay in the hospital 8-10 days after each treatment, went home for two weeks, and then the cycle started again. At the end of it all, she was miraculously healed, and our doctors declared her cancer-free!

While illness can be a lonely, grueling, and painful battle for the patient, caretaking can become a lonely, grueling, and painful battle as well. Most of the time, caretaking is just one more task to add to all the regular roles of family, work, and home. We have to learn to juggle, reorganize, and sometimes redefine what is most important.

One day I read the passage in 2 Corinthians 11 where the apostle Paul lists all the dangers he faced while serving God. After the list, Paul adds,

"I have worked hard and long, enduring many sleepless nights.... Then, besides all this, I have the daily burden of my concern for all the churches." (v. 27–28).

Caretakers do not face dangers (thank goodness), but along with all the other work that has to be done, we have hearts heavy with concern for our loved ones.

It's definitely a life change. A friend, Pam, recently shared this aspect of caretaking for her husband while he fought cancer:

"At first, I couldn't swallow to eat, and I would forget to eat. My focus every minute, day and night, was seeing to Paul's needs. Many days I had to cry out to God to give me strength to get through that day. I cried a lot and struggled with not letting fear overtake my mind."

I know every caregiver has felt those emotions. My panic time was when doctors first told us Melody had cancer. They didn't know what type or what stage, but they knew it was cancer. I remember going to a Starbucks near the hospital. I sat in the comfy chair for a couple of hours. I wrote page after page in my journal, and then I just sat there, emotionally worn-out. I couldn't see what was ahead. Was I going to lose Melody? Did God lift His hand? Was He going to leave me alone?

It was a horrible couple of hours. In the end, I knew I had to get up, dry my tears, and go back to help Melody. Just as she decided she wasn't going to waste this experience, I decided that even if Melody was going to die, I didn't want her ever to think that I didn't serve her, love her, and encourage her through this walk. Little did I know what all that really meant.

As I write this, I know that my job was nothing compared to many other caretakers. I rarely had messes to clean up, I wasn't beside Melody 24 hours a day, and I didn't have to hand-feed her.

I also had the hope of her being cured. However, I am convinced that the principles to help carry any caretaker through their responsibilities are the same. A caretaker has to realize that God sees their diligence, He hears their fearful thoughts, and He cares for them as a loving Father.

He Sees Your Diligence

The role of a caretaker is to do the things for a loved one that he or she can't do themselves; to provide for them what they can't provide themselves; to fight for them when they can't fight for themselves. Every day the caretaker cooks the meals, cleans the house, does the laundry, runs the errands, put gas in the car, pays the bills, picks up the medicine, fights with the doctors for proper care, and too many other things to list. While we are grateful to serve, it takes every ounce of diligence to keep things running.

It is easy for diligence to turn into frustration. I'm sure the apostle Paul constantly had to settle issues, meet needs of church members, preach yet another sermon, and after all that, write another letter. I'm also pretty sure that every now and then, he wanted to say, "I haven't healed from my last stoning! Think you can handle it?" I'm even more sure that he would bite his tongue, take the focus off his needs, and meet the needs of the church.

> *"So let's not allow ourselves to get fatigued doing good. At the right time we will harvest a good crop if we don't give up, or quit. Right now, therefore, every time we get the chance, let us work for the benefit of all, starting with the people closest to us." (Galatians 6:9–10 MSG).*

He knows that God is watching as he serves and cares for others and that God will remember it all.

"For God is not unjust. He will not forget how hard you have worked for him and how you have shown your love to him by caring for other believers, as you still do." (Hebrews 6:10).

God isn't aloof or unaware of our diligence. He holds us close, and He will reward us at just the right time. Even if we do mess up and get grumpy and tired and frustrated, God sees our weariness and helps us get back up. One time Melody asked me to go back to the kitchen I had just left for something else, and in my tiredness, I sighed a little louder than I intended. It hurt Melody's feelings, which crushed me! I quickly apologized and assured her it was just tiredness and nothing personal toward her. I cried out to God for help and later came across this promise:

"The Lord helps the fallen and lifts those bent beneath their loads." (Psalms 145:14).

The hospital was 45 minutes from our house. Every time I got out of my car to walk into the hospital or into the house when she was home, I would pause and say a simple prayer: "Lord, help me to be what Melody needs. Help me to lift her up, not act tired, even though I am, and be an encouragement to her." Sometimes I had to walk around the hospital's gift shop to shake off the cares of the day before I headed up. Somehow, God grabbed my hand and walked with me as I cared for her. He will do this for you as well. He sees your diligence, and He is proud of your faithful and loving caring.

He Hears Your Fearful Thoughts

I start work at 7 a.m. One morning, about 7:30 a.m., I felt my phone vibrating, looked down, and saw the hospital's caller ID. Melody was in for her sixth treatment. My heart skipped a beat, and I quickly answered. My heart leaped over some beats when the caller identified himself as the floor doctor. (They are the ones in charge; you are lucky to see them once every day.)

He said they were having trouble waking Melody up. Her vitals were good, but they went ahead and moved her to the ICU to run some tests. He finished by saying he thought it would be a good idea for me to come to the hospital. My mind was just short of panicking, and I wanted to say, "Duh! I'm on my way!" But in a calm voice I said I would be there in 20 minutes. I ran by my boss to say there was an emergency, and soon I was walking into the hospital.

Over the next four hours, they ran several tests. Melody was very unresponsive, though she occasionally broke through the fog to mumble something. Everything turned out fine; she had just been over-medicated. That afternoon, around 3 p.m., she woke up, saw me sitting there, and said, "Oh, hi honey." I chuckled to myself because I knew she had no idea of the scare she gave us all.

"Scared" is a mild word for the fear I had that morning. We were never really told what to expect or if the cancer was getting worse. As I rushed to the hospital that morning, I kept asking God, "Is this it? What will I do? Should the kids come? What if she crashes in front of me and I have to watch them work to save her life?" (Even now as I write about this, the fear of "what if" runs through me.) I couldn't act afraid; I had to listen and pay attention to the 20 doctors, interns, and students from every discipline surrounding my wife. (Okay, maybe just 10 doctors.) Melody was the buzz of the ICU because no one knew what was wrong. I had to push my fears aside and be her caretaker.

God hears our fears. He understands and knows why we have them. Instead of scolding us, "Hey, I'm God. Leave it to Me," He calms us with words like:

> *"When you're in over your head, I'll be there with you. When you're in rough waters, you will not go down. When you're*

between a rock and a hard place, it won't be a dead end—
Because I am God, your personal God." (Isaiah 43:2–3 MSG).

He is our personal God. He knows our situations, He knows our issues, and He knows our fears. And what He says is, "Hang in there. I'm here." My friend, Lisa, said that she felt God was telling her, "I got this, Boo!"

In the middle of Melody's crowded ICU room, the neurologist on duty said to me, "Hey, I've heard about her case! It's so rare." She then turned and asked, with a sense of disbelief, how we were able to have the two top doctors of the vast hospital system working on the same case. I immediately realized that God had preordained this doctor to be in this ICU on this specific day so that He could use her amazement to comfort me. Only God could have arranged for us to have this level of care. As caretakers, we need to be aware of these special God-moments and keep them close to our hearts.

Fear is natural in caretaking situations. I was afraid of a lot of things. Would Melody be able to walk again? Would she be weak and tired forever? Would her "chemo brain" ever leave? And, of course, would she live? While these were legitimate fears, my wife overcame all of them.

Many caretakers don't have answers to their fears. And in the rush of caretaking, we don't even have time to be afraid. Fear usually rushes in during the off-moments, as we try to rest or have a minute of quiet. Mine always came as I was driving home from the hospital. Fear makes us feel alone. It pushes us into the dark and leaves us hopeless. It causes us to think things will never change and that we will be stuck as caretakers forever.

Hope is the opposite of fear. Hope leads us to believe that one day everything will work out. We don't know what will happen, but we have the assurance that it will all be okay. Hope feeds us the courage to keep putting one foot in front of the other.

Faith builds hope in our lives. When we take our fears to our Father, He looks under the bed and in the closet and tell us that He ran the Boogie Man off! Faith is the confidence that we can trust God, that no matter what is ahead, we will make it.

He Cares for You as a Loving Father

My earthly father was a huge comfort to me during Melody's battle with cancer. I would call him after work, and we would talk through what was happening. My father had been a caretaker for my mother. She fought Alzheimer's for nine years. The last three of those years were especially difficult. His comforting voice would calm my fears, push away my doubts, and help me to carry on through another day.

The week before Melody's first cancer treatment, my dad suddenly passed away. I remember thinking, "Who is going to help me now? Who can I talk to that will help me like Dad helped me?" On the 2 1/2-hour drive home following his funeral, I was dreading all that was ahead. The very next day, Melody would enter the hospital, and our world would change even more.

As Melody slept in the passenger seat, I began to hear another voice talk to me. It was just as tender, just as loving, and just as encouraging as my dad's had been. My heavenly Father began reminding me that He loved me, that He understood my heart, and that everything would be okay.

> *"Casting all your cares [all your anxieties, all your worries, and all your concerns, once and for all] on Him, for He cares about you [with deepest affection, and watches over you very carefully]"* (1 Peter 5:7 AMP).

I was reminded that God had been the voice in my ear all along. It was His voice that told me to take Melody to the UT Southwestern Medical Center. It was His voice that helped me push past the "gatekeeper" doctor and request a specialist. It was His caring heart that "randomly" lined up the top neurologist and top cancer doctor to take our case.

Over and over, God has shown how He cares for me. It was His voice that led a friend to offer to set up a Facebook page for us. At first, I said no, but it was His voice through another friend that told me I needed to let people help me. That Facebook page became a lifeline of support. Over 1,500 people joined in to encourage us, calm our fears, and help us to make it through another day. It was His voice that led a group of coworkers to show their love and support by giving gift cards for food and gas to make the 45-minute round-trip drive every day. It was His voice that prompted two of my greatest mentors, Andy and Sarah Horner, to call me right as I was getting overwhelmed by the great task ahead. My dad may have been the initial voice of comfort and care, but God brought hundreds more to help us.

Please don't think that I was super spiritual during this time. While Melody prayed for all her medical caregivers, I struggled with a deep depression. With God's help, I kept it together pretty well in front of Melody. But behind the scenes, I struggled with a darkened heart. If God had not been such a loving Father to me—caring for me, helping drive my fears away, and strengthening me to be diligent—I surely would have lost all faith. He is a good, good Father.

He Has a Purpose to All of This Madness

To be honest, there were many times when I didn't care about anything other than making it through this battle with cancer. Yet as I read the comments on our posts and the cards that came in the mail, and as I visited with the select few we allowed in, I began to realize that we were encouraging others. People were finding faith in Christ, a marriage began to heal, and others were being encouraged to press through their own health issues. We were always surprised by the fact that those who were praying for us were also being encouraged by us at the same time.

Caregivers have little time to worry what others think. However, if they are faithful, trusting, and just don't give up, God will comfort them, and they will comfort others.

> *"All praise to the God and Father of our Master, Jesus the Messiah! Father of all mercy! God of all healing counsel! He comes alongside us when we go through hard times, and before you know it, he brings us alongside someone else who is going through hard times so that we can be there for that person just as God was there for us." (2 Corinthians 1:3–4 MSG).*

Caregivers must remember that God comes alongside us, cares for us, and leads us to comfort others. There's a great comfort in hearing that your fighting through fear and doubt and your faith in God has encouraged others.

Our greatest discouragements as caregivers come when we get focused on the daily grind of caring. We love our "patients," or else we wouldn't still be there. There's a sense of despair at times, I'm sure; the longer the struggle, the greater it can become. That's why we need to shift our eyes off our struggles and realize there is a much bigger purpose than we can see. If nothing else, it is to say to others, "God got me through that time, and He will get you through yours."

There were many times I would ask my dad questions like, "Why? Why did this happen to Melody and not me? What is the meaning behind this?" He would calmly answer each question the same way: "That's life." He would tell me that bad things happen in this world every day. Some people get sick, others not; some get healed, others die. God knew from before we were born what life would be like for us. My dad would sum up every conversation with encouragement:

It's not the good or the bad that we are to focus on; it's how we submit our lives to God. It's how we let God love us, care for us, and comfort us. And it's how we take His grace and share it with others. This is the ultimate advice for the tired caregiver. Let God carry you so that you can carry your loved one, and together, you can point others to trust in Him as well.

(For bonus material on caregiving and how to support a caregiver, visit www.MelodyBoxInspires.com/Caregivers.)

CHAPTER 9

"I'll think about that tomorrow. After all, tomorrow is another day."

Gone with the Wind

I've never seen a casket so small. I saw it in a picture on Facebook. Right next to the casket knelt a dad and his three-year-old son, grieving and comforting each other. Little Ivey only lived eight months in her mother's womb and then passed quietly from this world to her eternal home.

For Ivey's first four months, her birth was joyfully anticipated. For her last four months, her parents had to grieve the eventuality that if she lived through delivery, it would only be for minutes, possibly even seconds. Such heartbreaking darkness. Ivey's parents courageously posted on Facebook about their pain, their heartache, and their grief in those unimaginably difficult days. And in the same paragraph, they professed their hope and trust in God, that He hadn't left them and He is faithful, no matter how dark the journey.

One of the most poignant posts Ivey's mom wrote was about her sadness in realizing they would not be able to enjoy Christmas with their newborn. With her permission, I'd like to share with you what she wrote:

"As soon as those thoughts came, another one came, a verse:

'Your eyes saw my unformed substance; in your book were written, every one of them, the days that were formed for me, when as yet there was none of them.' Psalm 139:16 ESV

The phrase, *'days that were formed for me'* stuck out in my mind. It didn't say, *'the days that were not formed for me.'* I realized I was grieving and sad over days and events God didn't write for her. **We weren't having these days stolen from us, they were never ours.** It was almost like God was saying, I didn't give you 'those' days, but I've given you today." (Amanda Weaver, Iveyshope.wordpress.com)

Wow. What maturity in those words. They remind me of Elisabeth Elliot: "Today is mine, tomorrow is none of my business. If I peer anxiously into the fog of the future, I will strain my spiritual eyes so that I will not see clearly what is required of me now."[16] You don't have to look very far before you find someone else going through their own dark moment. Sometimes it's someone else's suffering that wakes you up to thank God that you aren't having to walk their path.

God Cares About the Details in Your Life

There have been so many times I wished I could write my own story. I feel pretty certain you would say the same thing. And if I can't write it, I'd at least like the ability to edit it. I'd edit out the bad things that have happened in my life and in the lives of those I love (betrayals, deaths, disappointments, illness, financial stresses, etc.). I'd erase the things that bring pain and suffering to others (drug dealers, the slave trade, child abuse, racism, terrorism). I guess I'd also need to take care of natural disasters that have negative effects on our world (earthquakes, hurricanes, tsunamis, droughts, forest fires, etc.). And then what would I do about the political and imperial arenas around the world? Come to think of it, God's job is hard! From a human standpoint, there is no way I could even scratch the surface of righting evil in this world, much less make everything right in my own small place in history.

"My thoughts are nothing like your thoughts," says the Lord. "And my ways are far beyond anything you could imagine. For just as the heavens are higher than the earth, so my ways are higher than your ways and my thoughts higher than your thoughts." (Isaiah 55:8–9).

And that's why I would make a poor God. God's thoughts, plans, ways, methods, and strategies are infinitely higher and greater than mine, and they are better in every possible way. They take me by surprise. They go beyond what I could ever dream or imagine. They surpass all my expectations. God accomplishes His plans as He takes into account every detail of history from start to finish. How awesome is that?

One of the things I love about the modern digital world is the ability to pull up a picture on my smart phone and zoom in for detail or zoom out for perspective. (I'm so used to it now that I've held a physical photo in my hand and found myself mindlessly trying to zoom in with my fingers!) That's how I imagine God viewing history. He can zoom in on my life and see the days when my hair was falling out due to the chemotherapy. Each day, He had a perfect account of how many hairs were left on my head.

"And the very hairs on your head are all numbered. So don't be afraid; you are more valuable to God than a whole flock of sparrows." (Luke 12:7).

God cares that much about you! When God says He has the hairs on your head numbered, He is saying that He is very interested in you and has intimate knowledge about you, your body, your family, your finances, your relationships—everything in your life. And His zoomed-in picture is never fuzzy, pixilated, or out of focus.

God cares as you struggle with the pain in your body that the doctors can't identify. He hears as you cry out to Him about that financial worry you've been keeping a secret from your family. He sees your faithfulness as you show up to work day after day to a boss who doesn't value you. He understands the deep hurts from the past you have buried down in your heart.

God wants you to know that if something concerns you, it concerns Him. He knows every problem you are worried about and every burden you are carrying. And when you approach Him for help, He has all the time in the world for you. In that moment, it's just you and Him, as if no one else exists. That is how valuable you are to Him and how in love He is with you.

About two months into treatment, I began hearing music in my head. Real music. Symphony music, radio music, piano music. Marching bands, choirs, rehearsal bands. Banjo music. The music was so real that I thought it was coming down the hall from my hospital room. I heard this music when I was sleeping, and I heard it when I was wide awake. I heard it when I was in the hospital and when I was at home. It was vibrant. It was beautiful. Even when the orchestra was warming up or the marching band had a little too much snare drum, I heard it all. Now, I knew it had to be in my head. There was no swing band practicing down the hall in the hospital, but the music was absolutely so real that sometimes I felt as if I was composing it.

I told a friend who was visiting me in the hospital about the music. I started hearing it again while she was there, and I asked her to please look in the closet to see if a nurse had a radio on in there. It was hard for me to comprehend that my friend couldn't hear it the music. She, of course, said she didn't hear any music, but she told me just to relax and enjoy it. God was sending His angels to sing over me. I loved that.

I remember seeing on a TV show that hearing things that aren't there can be an indication of a brain tumor. And since everything you see on TV is true, I began to think that maybe I had a brain tumor. I told Phil, and we decided to ask my neurologist about it at my next appointment.

At my next visit, I told my doctor about the music I was hearing. I thought for sure he was going to order an immediate MRI to find the tumor in my brain. He stopped typing into his tablet to listen, and he asked me a couple of questions. Then, he sort of shrugged his shoulders to indicate it was nothing to worry about and went back to typing into his tablet. So, I mentally shrugged my shoulders, too.

After that, I didn't hear the music for a while. I kind of missed it. Then one day as my nurse was checking me in and recording what medicines I had already taken and what medicines I still need to take, I started hearing the music again. This time it was the classic hymn "Because He Lives." I heard every word: "Because He lives, I can face tomorrow. Because He lives, all fear is gone. Because I know He holds the future, and life is worth the living just because He lives."[17] What a great song for God to instruct the angels to sing over me and my brain. I looked up at my nurse and smiled. I realized she didn't have a clue of what was happening in my head. I resigned myself to an MRI to find that tumor.

Without looking up, my nurse said, "Sounds like we've got some singing going on in the next room." I didn't know I had been holding my breath, but I exhaled and said, "Oh, do you hear that, too?"

Yes. There was singing going on in the next room.

God knew me. He knew I didn't have a tumor in my head. He also knew that I love music and that I might eventually enjoy that whole experience of hearing the music. To this day, I don't have an explanation of the music in my head, but whether there had been a tumor or not, I knew I could trust Him in His plan and purpose for me.

Maybe my experience of hearing music in my head is for you. I know it's for me because I enjoyed it, and I love telling people about it. It's a good anecdote. But I know God saw this day in my future. He knew I would have my fingers on the keyboard today, and He would bring this story to my mind. He also knew that one day YOU would be reading this book. Maybe this story would make you think about something playing in your mind. It might not be music, but it might be questions. Or it might be one question. *Is God real?*

Some of you may believe in the existence of God, but you aren't quite at the place of believing that He cares about the details of your life. Others of you may not believe in God at all. I can only think that you made it this far in the book because you are my friend. We know each other personally, and you wanted to hear more of my story. Thank you. Sincerely. Thank you for taking the time to read it. I am truly honored because I know you believe differently than me.

I have to be honest—I've had your face in my mind as I have written this book. I want you to know and experience God the way that I do, as a friend and Someone I can trust completely in the good times and the bad. If you aren't in a dark time right now, I'm glad. But dark times could be just around the corner. I want you to have Someone to lean on— Someone who wants the best for you and loves you more than I ever could. I want God to be as real to you as He is to me.

Maybe questions play like a broken record in your mind at night when things are quiet. If you are arguing with your-self about how someone could be so ignorant as to believe in something they can't see, it's my prayer that you do yourself a favor and do more research. Maybe your research starts with a simple prayer: "God. If you are there, then I know you hear me. If you are the God that Melody talks about, then I know You see me. So, if You hear me and see me, You know that I'm not sure if You are there. I'm going to pray that You show me You truly do care about me. I'm not going to dictate how You do that, but I'm going to watch for You to reveal Yourself to me."

Just start there. If your prayer is honest, if you really mean it, then I can guarantee that God will show Himself to you.

> *"When you come looking for Me, you'll find Me. Yes, when you get serious about finding me and want it more than anything else, I'll make sure you won't be disappointed." (Jeremiah 29:13–14 MSG).*

God will not hide from you. You don't have to be in a specific place or posture. You don't have to be cleaned up, and you don't have to have all your questions answered first. He says that when you look for Him, you will find Him. You can trust Him about that.

God Cares About the Design of Your Life

Not only can God zoom in on my life as if I was the only person on the face of the earth, but He can zoom out and see all the events that came before me and all the events that are coming after me. He sees the whole story of my life and how it fits into history and His plan for me. I imagine that it's kind of like the way we use the maps app on our smart phones. We can zoom out to see where we've been and where we are going. I haven't a clue how He does it, but while He sees and cares intimately for me, He sees and cares intimately for each and every one of you—at the exact same time and in the exact same way. It's just beyond comprehension. (He must have the smartest phone ever!)

God gave me the best parents in the world. Everyone loved them because of their kindness, their generosity, and their open and welcoming personalities. I learned so much about how to treat others just by watching them. They made me want to be like them. But whether I had wonderful parents (which I did!) or cruel parents or absent parents, it took the specific DNA from both my mother and my father to create me. In other words, if my mom had married someone else, I wouldn't be here today. God cared so much about me that He orchestrated both my parents' lives so that they would meet, fall in love, marry, and (voilà!) have me.

The genetics I inherited from my parents gave me a particular temperament. And that is why I am more of an introvert than an extrovert. Being an introvert doesn't mean I don't like to be around people or that I'm a hermit holed up in my home, pale-faced from avoiding the sun, allowing my fingernails to grow so long they clickety-clack on my keyboard. (That is an interesting visual!) (Don't worry, I don't look like that.) (Check out my picture on the back of the book.) (Parentheses are fun!) It just means that while I enjoy people, I get my energy and I recharge when I am alone.

However, being an introvert does mean that I've had to make a conscious effort to come out of my shell and give myself to people. That's why my life verse is Mark 8:35, *"If you try to hang on to your life, you will lose it. But if you give up your life for my sake and for the sake of the Good News, you will save it."* What that says to me is this: If I try to protect my life from people or close myself off from them, I will lose my life. But if I release my life and open up to others, that's when I will find life. The more I serve and freely give my time, attention and interest to others, the more I enjoy life and really live.

During the three weeks I was in rehab, I met many unhappy people living under a cloud of darkness. And to be honest, there were days that I preferred to stay in bed. I didn't want to go talk to the elderly lady who had broken a hip, or the middle-aged man recovering from a stroke, or the 20-something guy who had a massive head injury and was having to relearn how to do everything. But my therapists, who knew how hard it was for me just to swing my legs over the side of the bed and transfer into a wheelchair, were always so kind to encourage me to try. And I did try. Each day I rolled up to my group therapy circle and prayed for God to lift up my spirit so that I could give myself away and lift up someone else's spirit.

I think it was the second day in rehab that I rolled up to my group and introduced myself to the wheelchair-bound woman on my left. She was elderly and looked defeated and cranky. She told me her name and answered my other questions about how long she had been in rehab and what brought her there. After she told me all about herself, her family, her pets, and when she was going home, we sat in silence looking at our feet. Finally, she abruptly broke the silence and asked me, "What are you in for?" I just said, "Cancer." She shook her head and said, "That's a rough one." Then the lady on our right shouted out, "Cannabis!"

All-righty then.

We had group therapy twice a day, which mostly consisted of getting our wheelchairs in a circle and tapping our feet to music and strengthening our arms by lifting light weights. I did my best to smile at every person and talk to the people on my immediate right or left. I wish I could say that my smile and pleasant conversation turned the whole group dynamic into one happy family that looked forward to seeing each other every day, but it didn't. On my last day, they all gathered around me, and we sang a hymn. (Nope. That didn't happen either.)

But just because you don't see God at work doesn't mean He is absent. God's design for my life is to glorify Himself through my temperament. My temperament is one that prefers to be by myself, but with God working inside me, I make decisions daily to open myself up and experience real and abundant life as I give myself away and serve others. Even though I prayed with many while I was in rehab, I have no idea what happened once I left and started on my chemotherapy in another hospital. But God does.

What if He pulled back the curtain and gave me a glimpse of what happened after that stay in rehab? What if He expanded the history timeline so that I could see not only what happened in 2014 and 2015, but what was going to take place years in the future? What if it looked something like this ...

Because the cancer damaged the nerves in my legs, I had to go to rehab to learn how to take care of myself when Phil was at work and I was home alone. While I was in that rehab hospital, only chosen because it was close to our home, I met a nurse who had lost her dad to cancer a few weeks earlier. I spent some time talking with her and encouraging her to start going back to church to find comfort in her grief. I was released from the hospital and never saw her again.

A few weeks later, the nurse and her husband, who was a medical technician, decided to give church another try. On the weekend they attended, the pastor announced a medical mission trip for volunteers to work two weeks in some of the most impoverished villages in the island communities of Indonesia. The church was in desperate need for medical professionals, and this young couple felt moved to use some of the small inheritance from her dad's estate so they could both go on the trip. While in Indonesia, they fell in love with the people and enjoyed their work so much that they decided to stay an additional two weeks.

In those last two weeks, they met a young man who had always wanted to come to America to finish his education in the medical research field, and all he needed was a sponsor. The nurse and her husband sponsored him, enabling him to complete his education in America. Over the next several years, this young man was instrumental in tremendous advancements in treatments for blood cancers like leukemia and lymphoma, and the survival rate for children rose to well over 85%.

One of the children who benefited from this research and without it most certainly would not have survived, went on to graduate from college with an agricultural degree. He was hired by a company to use his skills to develop vertical farming in urban areas where year-round crop production could take place, feeding the world's most impoverished areas. A prominent leader in one of the areas benefitting from this new way of farming was so impressed with the results that she began traveling and raising money to enable more communities to access this innovative approach to food production and supply. She started a foundation and was so passionate about this project that she was able to influence and enlist seven of the wealthiest people in the world to be on her board and manage the funds raised. These funds raised were used to virtually eradicate world hunger. One of the board members was impressed to do some press conferences around the world, and at the press conference in Japan …

Should I go on? Do you understand the picture I am trying to paint? Am I saying God gave me cancer? No! Cancer is bad, and the things in this world that make us sad (child abuse, disease, homicide, etc.) make God sad. In heaven, things will be perfect. I'm convinced that we've lived in imperfection so long and so comfortably that we will be blown away by God's definition of perfection. It will be beautiful. It will be delicious. It will feel better than any single millisecond that we've ever felt on earth.

But we aren't in heaven yet. We are still on earth, where things are not perfect. While we are here, God can take bad things and bring good out of them.

"And we know that God causes everything to work together for the good of those who love God and are called according to his purpose for them." (Romans 8:28).

Ev-ery-thing. You may ask, "Even birth defects?" God says, "I take responsibility for the birth defects because I have a bigger perspective than you. I have a greater plan than you. I can see what you can't see." Do you think God loves a hearing person more than a deaf person? Of course not! But because His ways are higher than mine, I can trust Him to know what He is doing. You might say, "I know the Bible says 'everything,' but what about my mom who has suffered from Alzheimer's for the last ten years? She doesn't know me or any of her loved ones. Surely God doesn't want that for her." No, He doesn't. It hurts His heart as much as it hurts yours. Since my thinking is not like His, I don't know what His plan is. I do know that I can trust Him to take this terrible thing and bring good out of it.

Phil and his mom had a difficult relationship most of his life. While he knew beyond a doubt that she loved him, he never remembers a time that she told him she was proud of him. He always received the message that he was "less than" when they were together. It was sad, and it hurt my heart for him. Phil's mom developed Alzheimer's and lived with this debilitating disease for nine years. But it was in the midst of this disease that Phil felt the most love and acceptance from his mom. She lost the capabilities of her mind in regular things, but it was as if God allowed Phil to have a peek at what his mom would be like when God decided to bring her to her eternal home. I can see the way she smiled and looked at him in my mind's eye right now. She loved him, respected him, admired him, and her face showed it. Before this disease, I don't ever remember a time she looked at him that way.

One moment seared in my mind is a time we were saying goodbye following our afternoon visit. She hugged each of the kids and me, and when she was hugging Phil, she said, "You sure have some good kids, Phillip." He said, "Well, it's not because of me. It's because of your prayers, Momma." She kept hugging him and said, "No, Phillip, it's because you are a good dad. You've always been a good boy."

Well, naturally, this caused all of us to burst into tears. Those were the words Phil craved his whole life. Even though not everyone gets a "happy ending" story like that, this is a perfect example of how God brings good out of bad."

God Cares About the Development of Your Life

You've heard this phrase many times: "We are all just a work in progress." And this is true. I would still be in a wheelchair if my doctor hadn't asked me, "Now why are you still in that wheelchair?" I gave him a wisenheimer answer: "Um … because I had cancer." (I've actually never used the word *wisenheimer* before. I like it.) He just looked at me and said, "You need to get out of that wheelchair."

The real reason I was still in a wheelchair was because I had gotten used to it. I knew how to do everything I needed to do from it. I didn't want to do the work it would take to get out of it. I felt safe; falling out of my wheelchair wasn't nearly as scary as falling from a standing position.

But he was right. I needed to get out of that wheelchair, which was easier said than done. You'd think it was just a matter of standing up and putting one foot in front of the other. Unfortunately, no.

I had nerve damage from the cancer in both my feet and all the way up to my knee in my left leg. The nerve damage makes it feel like you are walking on water balloons. It can also cause a tingling feeling in both feet similar to the sensation of a foot waking up after it has fallen asleep. My left foot suffers from what is called "drop foot" or "foot drop." I am not able to lift my toes or my foot. It just hangs there. I have lovingly named her "Flipper." Flipper will not go away. She will be with me for the rest of my life, which is why she has a cute name.

I had to re-learn to walk. And I did it! It wasn't easy, but I can't tell you how great it feels to be out of the wheelchair and not need the walker or the leg brace, or even that cute sparkly cane. I walk with a different, slower gait now, but that's ok, too.

We all have choices to make in our lives. We can decide to stay where we are, saying, "Well, this isn't so bad," or we can move forward, even if it's scary. My question to you is this: if God has a better life for you, why would you stay stuck where you are? It may be hard to move forward, physically and emotionally, but that's why you keep your focus on God and allow Him to lead you every step of the way.

> *"So we fix our eyes not on what is seen, but on what is unseen, since what is seen [the problem] is temporary, but what is unseen [God's power] is eternal." (2 Corinthians 4:18 NIV).*

You might want to say to me right now, "But, Melody, it is so much easier to focus on the difficulties (the divorce, the diagnosis, the death of a dream, or the death of a loved one). I understand. Believe me, I do. But lingering in the darkness will only cause you to go deeper into depression. Make a decision to shift your perspective. Instead of asking, "Why me?", ask "What do I do with this, God?"

Have you ever thought that one way God will bring good out of your darkness is to help someone else who is going through the same thing? When Phil and I were younger and going through some personal difficulties and struggles, a very wise man said, "One day, you will be able to use what you are learning right now to help someone else going through the same thing." In all honesty, in that very moment, neither one of us cared much how our struggle could help someone else, we just wanted out of the darkness!

But he was right. God has used our trials, our failures, our pain to help people over and over again. What struggle in your life can be used to help someone else going through the same thing? Who better to help someone going through a marital betrayal than someone who has gone through a marital betrayal? Who better to help someone going through the pain of infertility than someone who has gone through that pain? Were you the only caregiver to a spouse who suffered a terminal and long-term, debilitating disease? Don't waste the lessons you learned through that horrible trial. Someone else needs to hear about the ways you saw light through the darkness because they are walking the exact same path.

If you are in a desperate and dark place right now, I'm so sorry. I wish I could hug you, and sit with you, and drink some hot tea with cream and sugar. And just be quiet.

The message of this book is that God loves you and cares for you, and *grieves with you* when horrible things happen. But then He does what no one else on this planet can do. He takes the darkness that surrounds you and brings good out of it for His glory. Embrace God's plan for your life. You may not see His hand clearly right now, but let me assure you, once again, of this truth—God sees you, God hears you, God cares about you and *He Can Be Trusted.*

ENDNOTES

[1]   Isaiah 41:10
[2]   Isaiah 41:13
[3]   Jeremiah 1:8
[4]   Daniel 10:12
[5]   Daniel 10:19
[6]   Matthew 10:31
[7]   Matthew 14:27
[8]   Luke 1:30
[9]   Revelation 1:17
[10] Genesis 29:32
[11] Genesis 29:33
[12] Genesis 29:35
[13] Warren, Rick. "Problems Force Us To Depend on God." Pastor Rick's Daily Hope. May 21, 2014. Accessed August 29, 2017. http://pastorrick.com/devotional/english/problems-force-us-to-depend-on-god.
[14] Barlow, Harold, writer. "I've Got Tears in My Ears from Lying on My Back in My Bed While I Cry Over You," Spotify, track 9 on Homer and Jethro, *Ooh, That's Corny*, Sony Music Entertainment, 1963.
[15] Romans 8:28 NKJV
[16] Elliot, Elisabeth. *Keep a Quiet Heart*. Grand Rapids, MI: Fleming H. Revell, 2006.
[17] Gaither, Bill and Gloria Gaither, writers. "Because He Lives," Spotify, track 5 on Gaither Vocal Band, *Reunited*, Gaither Music Group, 2009.

Thank you for experiencing Melody's story in *He Can Be Trusted*, now experience the course. At MelodyBoxInspires.com you'll find a **FREE** downloadable chapter-by-chapter Study Guide that is perfect for individual or small group study.

This easy to complete guide takes you deeper into discovering how God can be trusted in the darkest of times. With only a few questions covering each chapter, you will be able to take your time and meditate on the things God is saying to you.

Is someone near you a caregiver? Are you at a loss with the best way to show them that you care? Would you like to give practical and encouraging support to a caregiver in your church, community or family?

Or are *you* a caregiver, and you don't know what to answer when someone asks how they can help?

Phil and Melody have a gift for you. You can find a free downloadable guide called Caring for the Caregiver at MelodyBoxInspires.com. These tips were gathered from caregivers who have struggled with the same questions you might have.

You can find this and more at
MelodyBoxInspires.com.

AUTHOR, SPEAKER, COMEDIAN, ENCOURAGER

Like you, Melody Box, knows the importance of choosing the correct speaker. The moment Melody steps on your stage, you'll know you made the right decision to bring her to your event. Her fusion of real-life stories and her conversational style is engaging to her audience. Her authentic approach combined with superb content positions her as a top choice for many non-profits, women's groups and businesses. She customizes each message to complement the theme and objective of your event.

CONTACT MELODY TODAY TO BEGIN THE CONVERSATION AT MELODYBOXINSPIRES.COM.

CPSIA information can be obtained
at www.ICGtesting.com
Printed in the USA
FFHW010607020219
50378925-55505FF

9 781640 850460